Plague
of Darkness

Plague
of Darkness

*We hid in the dark of the root cellar
while the German soldiers and their dogs
moved noisily about the farmyard above us.*

A memoir by
Leah Peska Kabel

Wolfson Press
Indiana University South Bend

Cathedral photograph by Eugene Wei
Photograph of Julius Peska's painting
    on pg. xi by Joel Langston
Photo restorations and barn drawing
    by Pavel Eshanov
Photograph on pg. 84 by Kitkatcrazy
    at Wikipedia, Creative Commons
    license CC BY-SA 3.0
Book design by David James, Ken Smith,
    and Michael Kouroubetes

ISBN: 978-1-950066-01-8

Wolfson Press
Master of Liberal Studies Program
Indiana University South Bend
1700 Mishawaka Avenue
South Bend, Indiana 46615
WolfsonPress.com

Contents

Gertrude's Family

- Babbi Shoshanah Colman Knobloch, great-grandmother, was part
  of a group of residents of a home for the elderly taken by Nazis to the
  Theresienstadt concentration camp and never heard from again
- Mama Auguste and Tate Anton Jakub Phillip, grandparents, bought
  and improved a Cherry Hill property above the Elbe valley,
  guarded their Jewish heritage, and were secretly active in politics
  - **Mutti Gertrude Sara Peska was Leah's devoted mother
    and also an accomplished artist**
    - **Leah, the author**
  - Tante Minkl and her children hid in Stienek's barn with Leah's family
    - Cousin Ewald grew up to become a chess champion after the war
    - Cousin Mia's health was broken as an infant in a refugee camp
    - Cousin Martin was born after the war in West Germany
  - Tante Erna, the baker, secured the visas that made possible
    the family's escape from behind the Iron Curtain
- Onkel Hans, the dashing tailor, spoke out against the Nazi regime
  and was beaten to death by fanatics, then thrown into the river
- Tante Anna emigrated to Montevideo, Uruguay, before the war
- Tante Jenny died in her thirties of tuberculosis
- Tante Fanny disapproved mightily of Leah during the time
  the niece was her ward in New Jersey

Julius's Family

- Molly Richter Peska and Votta Joseph Peska, grandparents, supported
  Julius's education and cared for Leah as a child
  - Onkel Ferdinant died of malaria while sailing homeward after serving
    in Madagascar in World War I
  - Onkel Frantisec also served in World War I
  - Onkel Zeph served in World War I, survived the Nazi labor camps,
    and was reunited with the family after World War II
  - **Papa Julius Peska, Leah's father, was a journalist, artist, and scholar**
    - **Leah, the author**
  - Tante Margit died in the global influenza epidemic of 1918,
    just before she was to marry
  - Onkel Rudi died of typhoid fever contracted on a youthful hiking trip
- Karel Richter was Molly Richter Peska's prosperous brother
  - Onkel Franz, Karel's son, was probably forced to join the Nazi party
    but warned Leah's family that they must flee for their lives

- Pavel Peska was Votta Joseph Peska's brother
  - Cousin Stienek, Pavel's son, and wife Ludmilla risked everything
    to keep Leah's family safe from the Nazis on their farm
    - Jaro, Stienek's son, hid from the military press gangs
      beside Leah's family in the root cellar

The musician, the child, the poet, the adventurer,
the lovers, the herbalist, and the oarsman, from bow to stern,
painted by the author's father, Julius Peska.

Prologue

As I grow older, and as the future that lies ahead of me grows shorter, more and more of my thoughts turn to past experiences. It has taken nearly eighty years for me finally to come to terms with the past and the deficiencies and defects of the human race.

Each one of us is a product of our environment, and only through spiritual growth, high moral standards, strength in unison with humility, and regard for others can we ever hope to improve ourselves and elevate the quality of life for our descendants.

> That which had been lost
> has come from the past
> and it is to the past
> one must turn to find it.

Those words were written by Oskar Rabinowitz. He was one of the many famous German-speaking Czechoslovakian Jews of Prague, an extraordinary author of many books, of which a great number included research into the remarkable thousand-year-old Jewish community of Czechoslovakia.

I know of few documents that can confirm the precious letters and notes I still have from my parents that describe the tragedies and triumphs that befell the members of my family, but I will try to weave a narrative of those events to the best of my knowledge and recollection and tell our story of the time before, during, and since World War II. In the process of translating the Yiddish, German, and Czech notes that my dear parents of blessed memory entrusted to me, I may lose their essence and their compassion.

The *Wortschatz*, that is, the vocabulary words in use and the verbal imagery, unfortunately, are not as rich in the English language as in the Yiddish, German, or Czech tongues of that place and time. In addition, in this narrative I will be looking at the world not only through the eyes of my parents but through mine as well.

One of my earliest memories, at about age two-and-a-half, is of being wheeled in my carriage past a medieval church in my home town of Krasne Bresno, in Czechoslovakia. I can still hear horses' hooves clattering on the ancient cobblestones, pulling a frightening black hearse in the direction of the cemetery. Dark-cloaked, veiled silhouettes walked silently behind it. A solitary bell, the *Totenglocke*, the bell for the dead, was ringing in the church tower. "*Shhh, zein still,*" I was told in Yiddish. I held my breath. The sadness and loneliness of this memory afflicted all the years of my childhood, and that scene recurred in my dreams throughout my life. Again and again, I saw that hearse in dreams before or after facing a frightening experience, and as an adult, I had periodic nightmares of that drama in the years that came after.

Little did I know in 1936 that Hitler and his henchmen were already plotting to annihilate the Jewish people. How could we have imagined that the tentacles of his regime would reach out as far as our unassuming little Bohemian town of Schönpriesen, *Schön* meaning beautiful, where the Jews in the Elbe Valley had lived relatively undisturbed for over one thousand years.

Chapter 1
The Creation of the Bohemian Jew

BECAUSE I AM A DISCIPLE OF ROMANTICISM, I am drawn to a fable once told to me:

The origin of the Slavic people

When Rome crumbled, the Germans returned to the province of Bohemia and later were joined by the Christian Slavic people in the eighth century.

According to legend, a patriarch by the name of Czech, who migrated from the Central Asian steppes of perhaps Kazakhstan or Chechnya, led his followers in search of a Promised Land, across vast steppes and the three great rivers, until they came to a hill of peculiar shape. His granddaughter, Elise, envisioned the city of Prague there, "whose domes shall touch the stars."

From that summit, Czech announced to his tired companions that they had reached at last the Promised Land, a land of endless forests, sparkling rivers, rolling hills, and green meadows wet with milk and honey.

In addition, there are records of Jewish merchants arriving from the Byzantine Empire into the area of Bohemia in the year 962 and again in 1092. During that era, the Byzantine populace had the foresight that their mighty empire was weakening, due to the approaching threat of the Ottoman masses, who were the enemy of the western, Christian-observant Byzantine culture.

The Christian and Jewish Byzantine inhabitants gradually migrated north into Serbia and west to Romania and the regions of the Austro-Hungarian Empire, where they found shelter in the town of Pilsen, Bohemia, and the districts of Moravia and Silesia. Prince Radoslav welcomed and requested Jewish Orthodox teachers from the Byzantine Empire to live in the provinces of Bohemia, Moravia, and Silesia because he wanted to dwarf the effect of the western Christian influence of Salzburg and Passau.

Although these efforts largely failed, the Jewish people never left the Slavic regions. Together with the Byzantine Christians, who were humanistic, charitable, and philanthropic in nature, we helped to create the appealing Bohemian character.

Saint Wenceslaus, a figure of legendary kindness and goodness but also of history, was born in Prague in 912. After the fall of the Roman Empire, the area which comprised northern Europe was leaderless, secretive, poverty-stricken, and corrupt. Wenceslaus ruled Bohemia and Moravia from 924 or 925 until 935, when he was murdered by his younger brother. Immediately after his death, he was considered a martyr and a saint, a bright light illuminating an obscure future. Statues in his honor and town squares named after him are still to be found all over the Czech Republic. His birthday is celebrated on the twenty-sixth of December.

Eventually, the Jews acquired more and more recognition and no longer thought of themselves as aliens in a strange land. They were slowly adopted by the Bohemian, Moravian, and Silesian culture and eventually began to slide into assimilation just as we did in the "melting pot" of America.

The German population in the eleventh century was busy with pogroms and brutalities against the Jews and forced them to move east to Poland, Austria, Bohemia, and Moravia, where they found at least temporary shelter. The riots against the Jews continued in Germany, and by the thirteenth century hundreds of Jewish communities were destroyed, and at least 100,000 Jews were murdered.

But that was only the prelude to the destruction of German Jewry during the spread of the Black Death, the plague that engulfed western Europe in the fourteenth century. The Jews were accused of causing that pestilence by poisoning the wells. The tradition of washing our hands before we eat may have saved many of us from contracting that hideous disease.

In addition, Bohemia became a haven to thousands of Spanish Jews fleeing their country in the fifteenth century because of oppression and persecution during the period of the Inquisition. Hence the term "wandering Jew" was used in an insulting manner in Christian Europe as, time and time again, our people were driven east to Bohemia, Moravia, Hungary, and Poland.

In the year 1620, the Bohemians lost their independence. The Hapsburg Empire dominated the Czech nation from then until 1918 and, as a result, the society became Germanized. Everyone asks me why we spoke German instead of Yiddish in our home. In fact, the Czech language was only heard in out-of-the-way villages in Bohemia. In Slovakia and Hungary, however, that was not the case. Those provinces were then controlled by Hungary.

In time, an elite group of Jewish citizens belonged to the distinguished Prager club, individuals such as Freud, Kafka, Goethe, Heinrich Heine, Oskar Karp, Gustav Stern, Theodor Herzl, Chaim Weitzmann, Thomas Mann, and let's not forget Rabbi Moses Schreiber and Rabbi Teitelbaum. Rabbi Teitelbaum stayed in Bohemia until 1942, helping Jews to hide out in Christian homes or flee to Switzerland.

A Bohemian is a German, a Czech, or a Jew by nationality living in the province of Bohemia. The Bohemians originally were a nomadic tribe that migrated from the outer borders of India and Iran and settled in Bohemia around the year 1000. Thus, the Slavs, the Jews, and the Bohemians were rocked in the same cradle, so to speak.

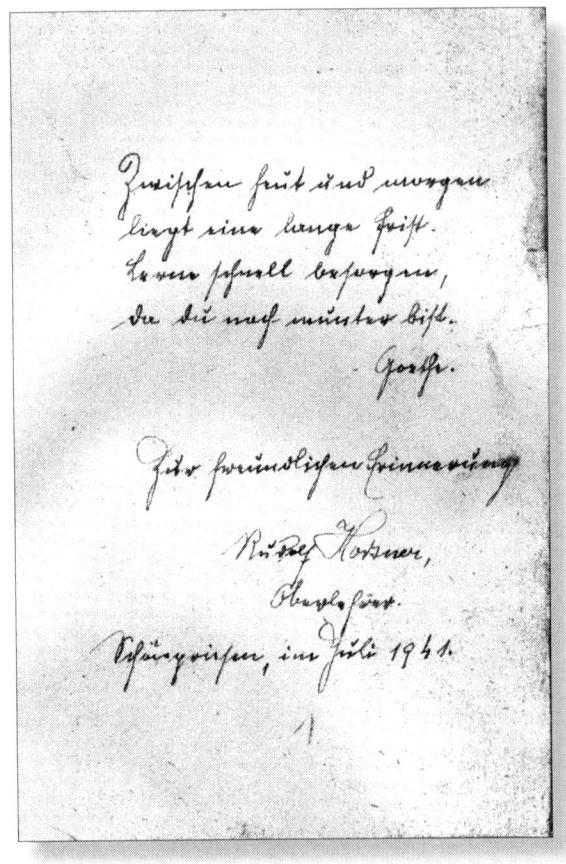

In the handwriting of my teacher,
Headmaster Rudolf Hossner:

Between today and tomorrow,
there is a long interval.
Quickly learn to provide
while you are still wide awake.

Goethe

Chapter 2
Romanticism vs. Realism
for the Bohemian Individual:
Felix Weltch's Description of the Bohemian Jew

ROMANTICISM CAN SUGGEST a specific trend toward the arts and can be found in the creative personality. This type of romanticism is not one of fantasy, illusion, or neurosis, but one that takes reality into account. Realism, on the other hand, is not influenced by irrational views and illusions. The realist measures, calculates, and observes through psychological and sociological means, and when it comes to his own person, observation turns into self-analysis. That sort of realism can promote honesty with oneself and, as a result, may eventually make mankind's liberation possible from the dilemmas, the *tsoris*, the problems, it usually finds itself in.

We can deduce that a Realistic Romanticism is found in the creative personalities in Bohemian, Moravian, and Czech Jews, as well as in Christians. Just to mention a few leading figures as an extension to the descriptions of the Bohemian character we have seen in the previous chapter, there was Gustav Mahler, a brilliant Jewish composer, whose creative works became world-famous. There was Antonin Dvorak's well-known *Ninth* or *New World Symphony*. Bedrich Smetana, born in Bohemia, composed his most inspiring piece, "Die Moldau," in 1874, when the country later known as Czechoslovakia was bursting with patriotic passion. It is not surprising that the Czech Zionists adopted those soul-stirring notes as the melody of the Israeli national anthem, *Hatikvah*, "The Hope," for they too were ecstatic with patriotism.

There was the famed Franz Kafka, a writer from Prague, whose major theme was "Man's unfathomable relationship with God." In the case of Max Brod, we see both realism and romanticism in his works, as in *Tycho Brahe's Path to God* and his famous *Reubeni, Prince of the Jews*. Franz Werfel, a poet from Prague, overflowed with emotion and humility, and yet he had a sharp eye for reality. Egon Kirsch, the son of an old Jewish family in Prague, wrote romantic reports of realistic everyday life. Sigmund Freud grew up in Moravia, and though his opinions are no longer in vogue, he was one of the world's great psychoanalysts and said to be a person of *emes*, absolute truth, and realism.

And again we must marvel at the potential the Bohemian Jews offered the world, whether they were secular or religious. We can identify geniuses like Albert Einstein, Sigmund Freud, Franz Buber, Karl Arnstein, Marie Schwolken, Eva Landsberg, and Ludwig Singer. And I will address our world-famous rabbis and the religious organizations of that region in the pages to come.

Bohemian Jews had to face many challenges. They lived not only amidst, but also with, the religious, social, and political parties of other nationalities, which made them decidedly different from, for instance, German Jews. As a result of always having to look behind the scenes, they became experts at social criticism and psychology.

In this manner, our ancestors, living in the middle of Europe for centuries amongst Germans, Czechs, Slovaks, Hungarians, the Romani people (who we knew then as Gypsies), Catholics, Protestants, rabbis, atheists, capitalists, socialists, and Communists, achieved a realistic outlook on life.

This made them not only critical, but fortunately, and in some cases unfortunately, very open-minded. As a result, the contributions of German philosophers and poets, as well as Czech thinkers, appealed to the Jewish people. My grandparents and my parents were influenced by the ideas and ideals of their era. Masaryk, Einstein, Weiniger, Fichte, Heine, and many others left an impact on the German-speaking Jews of Bohemia.

Chapter 3
Humanism and Skepticism

BELIEF IN HUMANISM AND SKEPTICISM concerning the medieval practices of the Roman Catholic Church took root early in the Bohemian lands.

The most outspoken and powerful leader of this movement was Jan Hus. He was extremely popular with the Czech population, especially with the university crowd. His assaults on the Catholic Church were so effective that the leaders of the church had him burned at the stake in the year 1415. Because Hus had so many followers, the Catholic Church launched five crusades to defeat the Hussites, and over the next two centuries, the Hussites fought back. The ensuing war between the Hussites and the German Roman Catholics makes Jewish history in the Czech lands somewhat different from the chronicles of Jews in other parts of Europe.

The Hussites formed a Czech Protestant movement and, unlike German Protestants and Roman Catholics, they did not view Jews as anti-Christian. In fact, rabbinical authorities during that period wrote sympathetically about the *B'nai Hussim*, the Sons of Hus.

After the Protestants were defeated in the seventeenth century, the Slavic or Czech culture was driven underground by the Catholics. Some Czechs were executed, and thousands were expelled from their lands. They compared their exile to the Jewish Diaspora. Faced with the choice of expulsion, some converted to Catholicism, and many converted to Judaism, a step that is rare in Jewish history.

But the saga of Jan Hus does not end here. Despite the fact that the Hussites lost to the Catholic Church, Jan Hus's ideology of Humanism and Skepticism never diminished. Even under the Austro-Hungarian Empire and a long line of Kaisers, there were no pogroms and very few attacks against the Jewish population anywhere there during the Austro-Hungarian dynasty.

Tomas Masaryk continued that tradition when in 1918 he established the Republic of Czechoslovakia after the crumbling of the Austro-Hungarian Empire. Masaryk's motto was "Equal Rights" for all eighteen resident nationalities, which included 380,000 Jews as well as 450,000 Romani. The Jewish population flourished academically and spiritually under his reign until Adolph Hitler's annexation of the Czech lands in the year of 1939.

The Dangers of Broadmindedness

There were two kinds of Jews in Czechoslovakia. The first kind was well-educated. They spoke both Czech and German, sent their children to *gymnasia*, high schools, and universities, and lived a secular life. Most had stopped observing Jewish law and did not appear much different from the non-Jewish population.

They educated their children to believe that Prague and Vienna belonged to them too, and in this atmosphere of contentment and stability, every citizen became cosmopolitan, a *Weltmensch*, a global citizen. It was a keen internal desire of the Jews to adapt themselves to the environment of the country, a longing for a homeland, for inclusion, for peace.

The second kind of Jew continued living on the *Judengasse*, the Jewish lane, within walking distance of the synagogue. They observed Shabbat and the Jewish holidays and spoke not only Czech and German but Yiddish as well.

The most challenging issue was finding a proper balance between loyalty to one's heritage on the one hand and open-mindedness on the other. I wish there had been a formula for achieving a balance between the two.

I can see the negative results that open-mindedness toward other cultures encourages when it becomes so great that you lose your culture and individuality in the process. For centuries, Jews in America, the melting pot of the world, have faced these challenges and, as a result, have in some cases had to face disastrous consequences through intermarriage and through assimilation.

As I am still searching for answers, I find it necessary, before continuing my memoirs, to look into the circumstances that influenced the behavior of especially the young Jewish population of that period in Bohemia. Foremost, as mentioned before, these Jews are a result of their environment. Very important also are all the tendencies that people inherit from their ancestors. Also important are the geographical, economic, and political conditions under which they live, their habits, their education, and most important, their religious consciousness.

Many decades ago, the lives of the older generation were carefully regulated by daily prayers, the celebrating of Jewish festivals, and observance of the Commandments. All that was tradition and Realism, and that it is how it was for many centuries. One did not even consider the path of Romanticism.

The nineteenth century brought great upheaval with *Haskala*, Enlightenment, scientific thought, the Industrial Revolution, closer contact with the neighbors, and social advancement. All these positive issues gradually led to a weakening of religious beliefs, especially in Germany, Bohemia, Moravia, and Silesia.

The City of Prague

We must also not forget the psychological influence of the city of Prague on the youngsters of the region. I should mention that Prague established the first university in Europe in 1348. This fact surely reflected the values of the Bohemian culture, which in my opinion was greatly influenced by the presence of our Jewish faculty.

Worthy of mention also is that under the Austro-Hungarian monarchy, as well as under President Masaryk's Czechoslovakian government, the education of its citizens was taken seriously. Cultivating good character, such as rules of conduct, moral obligations, modesty, and accountability, was insured by a subject called *Sittenlehre*. Moral ethics and philosophy were taught in the public school system, and all public schools were segregated into girls' and boys' sections.

The city of Prague was the spiritual and political center of Bohemia, Moravia, and Silesia. Few cities awakened a sense of history and Romanticism as did Prague. Just consider the impression of wonder or awe that I as a child had when we visited Josephstadt, a mostly Jewish-populated part of the city, to get reacquainted with our relatives, the Fischer family, just before World War II. I believe Mr. Fischer was a journalist and a publisher.

The oldest part of Prague, dating from the thirteenth century, contains the most architectural relics of Bohemian grandeur. Even during the Nazi occupation, despite the fear and anxiety one was perpetually under, one couldn't ignore the splendid mansions, then no doubt inhabited by German military personnel. Those mansions certainly suggested visions of a glorious past, as did the strangely meandering narrow streets, which lost themselves in dark mysterious corners; the quiet old courtyards of aristocratic airs; the many Gothic and Baroque churches of which Saint Vitus, the cathedral atop Hradcany, the Castle District, was the architectural summit of the city.

Many rich *mysehs*, tales, spin around the Jewish landmarks of the city of Prague, the imposing, elegant *Alt-Neu Shul*, and the mysterious ancient Jewish cemetery that sent chills up and down the spine. And let's not forget the legend of the Golem of Prague, the giant who was supposed to have been created by Rabbi Loew to help protect the Jews from the many calamities attempted by anti-Semites. Rabbi Yehuda Loew, better known as the Maharal, was a brilliant thinker and one of the most renowned scholars in medieval Jewry. He speaks of the dignity of man and of his central position in the hierarchy of existence. I especially find inspiring the statement in which he implies that man's excellence is not a gift with which he comes into this world:

> It is rather a development which he must achieve through
> his own efforts. As formed by the creator, a man is incomplete,
> and the whole burden of his life is a striving for completion,
> a quest for perfection.

Such a statement makes you take a good look at yourself, doesn't it? The Maharal became a legendary figure not only for the Jews but for the other inhabitants of Prague as well, for at least as long as the Jewish community was in existence.

You can see why the romantic aura of Prague reached out far into Bohemia, Moravia, Slovakia, Hungary, and even Austria. It inspired poets, artists, and scholars, both religious and secular. It was not surprising that the young people of Czechoslovakia had receptive minds and impressionable hearts.

Shoshanah Colman Knobloch
was taken by Nazis in 1942,
never to be found again.

Chapter 4
My Grandparents
and Great-Grandparents

I WILL NOW BEGIN TO REVEAL the memories and stories of six generations of Bohemian Jews, their failures and their triumphs, as I have learned from notes and stories, believed to be true, by my dear mother, father, grandparents, and great-grandmother. Not until recently did I realize that I misspelled my great-grandmother Shoshanah's last name. I was under the impression that it was "Kolman," but I was wrong. I found my great-uncle's name in *The Book of the Jews of Czechoslovakia*. Hugh Colman was one of the founders of the Joseph Pappen Lodge of the B'nai B'rith. A Zionist organization of the "Sons of the Covenant," it was established in 1928 in Marienbad, Bohemia, was destroyed by the Nazis in 1939, and was then revived in New York City in 1961. It had its worldwide meetings in Marienbad until 1938. I thought for a time that Hugh Colman was married to Shoshanah, but that is not correct. He was too young for her. Perhaps he was a brother or a cousin?

I have only a few recollections of my great-grandmother Shoshanah Colman of blessed memory. I don't know much about her heritage, but it appears that her parental home instilled excellent Jewish values. She was an observant lady. She covered her hair in the presence of rabbis, kept a kosher home, had separate dishes for meat and milk, as well as a few very special ones for *Pesach*, Passover. This had

*Anna, Mama's sister, migrated
to Montevideo, Uruguay, in 1914.*

to be a very admirable commitment for a woman of modest means. Not much is known about her parental home, but apparently her mother instilled Jewish values. Because my great-grandmother was impoverished, it was amazing that she had all this separate china for meat, milk, and, in addition, very special ones for Passover. Perhaps she inherited them, passed down from one generation to another? A set of china—much less three sets—and in addition, flatware, must have been quite expensive under the Austro-Hungarian Empire and the Czechoslovakian government.

My great-grandmother was married and widowed a few times, and this is where it gets a little confusing. Her first marriage produced no children. I know she bore daughters to her second mate, Mr. Knobloch: Anna, Auguste, Fanny, and Jenny. My great-grandfather died of heart failure, and one year later, Shoshanah married a widower with three children. As I said, I am confused myself because I don't know when Shoshanah's first husband died. And then

Jenny, Mama's other sister, age 35, in
Czechoslovakia. She died of tuberculosis.

there was a third husband by the name of Spec, Onkel Hans's father. Unfortunately, I wasn't given enough information about my grandfathers. Either they were not memorable enough, or they weren't around long enough. The Babbi *oben*, as we referred to her, which meant she was now in heaven, lived in Teplitz-Schönau in the province of Bohemia.

She very loyally raised her stepsons Hugo and Max Osterman, who in about 1914 migrated to Brazil, as did her stepdaughter Hilda. Her oldest daughter, Tante Anna, emigrated to Montevideo, Uruguay, and Tante Fanny to Camden, New Jersey. Her youngest daughter, Tante Jenny, passed on from tuberculosis early in life in our hometown. The Viennese disease, as they called it then, was rampant during those years. Yes, the post-World War I conditions were very bad. Not enough nutritious food meant low resistance to bacteria, and bad health practices, no access to health care, and, in addition, low fuel supply all caused the Viennese disease to spread quickly.

Yohanan Spec, whom the family called Hans, an offspring of the third marriage, was killed by the Nazis in 1941. So my precious grandmother, our Mama, as she was known to everyone, may she rest in peace, was to be in charge of the continuance of our Jewish successors.

My grandmother did not have an easy childhood. Shoshanah's third and fourth husbands died prematurely as well, and every time she lost a spouse, some of her children were taken to an orphanage, or perhaps it was the poorhouse.

But Shoshanah was a resilient, resourceful lady and she eventually opened a *Schneidergeschaft*, a tailor shop, in her home. During the harvest season, she also sold fruit at the marketplace, which grew abundantly in the Elbe valley. She obviously was very frugal as well. She and the children picked up the pieces of coal that fell off the freight trains onto the railroad tracks. Filling their buckets with the precious pieces of black gold, they used to heat their home for days. I can only imagine that the children no doubt enjoyed that activity. I can see my Mama—my grandmother—and her sisters skipping joyously along the railroad tracks, gathering the precious pieces of "black gold."

I remember the tall smokestacks of the Mars sugar factory and assume their source of energy and that of the rest of the population was wood and coal-burning stoves and furnaces. On cloudy days its fumes and the smoke darkened the Elbe valley, hence reminding us of the Biblical plague of darkness. As well, the dozens of locomotives that huffed and puffed day and night carrying and transporting goods and merchandise of all sorts in and out of the city increased the pollution. In contrast, on sunny days the smog disappeared into the horizon, and you could clearly see the pirates' fortress of Schreckenstein and the foothills of the Ore Mountains in the distance.

Despite the fact that every now and then Shoshanah was economically unstable, she had high standards in every way. One should be aware that not always has one thing to do with the other. In my mother's notes, she states that the Babbi read to them from the *Chumash*, the Torah, every time she visited, and she treated them to classical concerts and Yiddish theater.

Amselgrund—Blackbird Estate

My grandmother, Auguste Knobloch Phillip, was married early in life to a *sheyner Jud*, a dashingly handsome man, who sported a handlebar mustache. His name was Anton Jacob Phillip. His friends called him Tony. He served as a lieutenant in the Austro-Hungarian army under Kaiser Franz Joseph. Hundreds and thousands of Jews fought for Austria-Hungary in the First World War, which ironically would join forces with Hitler, who twenty years later slaughtered about one hundred thousand of them.

While my grandfather, our *Tate,* was in the service, my grandmother, whom everyone called Mama, delivered milk in the early morning hours before her children awoke. They lived on the Rosengasse in the

Anton Jacob Phillip, Leah's grandfather, a lieutenant in the Austro-Hungarian Army under Kaiser Franz Joseph, the tall man fourth from the right in the front row, marked with an X at his feet. He fought on the Balkan, Serbian, Romanian, and Russian fronts. He was a free spirit and believed in equality for all men. He belonged to the Bund, the Jewish Workers' Association, and the Hevra Kadisha, a Jewish Burial Association.

Ghetto, south of the tracks, near the Elbe River. My mother had many fond memories of living in the Jewish quarter of Krasne Chemnitz.

On the High Holidays, they attended services in the Shteibel at the rabbi's house. The Shabbat meals with Babbi, my great-grandmother, Tante Jenny, and Onkel Hans were always fun-filled, *heimish*, and cozy. (Heimish comes from the root word "Heim," the German word for home. So heimish was "informal, cozy, warm.") The children played with their dreidels in the streets, and the exchange of *nosh*, treats, with the neighbors at Purim time was memorable to my dear mother of blessed memory. Nosh is a snack, a small portion of food we gave to our neighbors on the holiday of Purim (the Feast of Esther) as an act of *chesed*—kindness.

My grandmother with Gertrude Sara
and Minkl Miriam.

When my Tate finished his duty under the monarchy, his young wife and mother of his three daughters surprised him with a *packel* of *kronen*, a sack of dollars that she had frugally saved from her milk money. Their dream had always been to break away eventually from the ghetto life and buy a plot of land on the Kirschberg, the Cherry Hill, appropriately named because it was bedecked with black cherry trees. The Elbe Valley was famous for its fruit orchards. And with the help of Shoshanah's frugal savings, they were able to purchase a property there.

Leopold Rompert, a famous Jewish journalist from a remote village in the province of Bohemia, said: *"You need a soul free of anxiety in order to listen to the sound of a bird. Anyone who enjoys the smell of a fir tree and the tantalizing lyric of a lark should not live in the ghetto."*

The desire to live side by side with the Czechs and the Germans was modish, in vogue, then. The inhabitants in the region wanted to share their ideas and their ideals. Under the newly established Republic of Czechoslovakia, headed by Tomas Masaryk, everyone was ready for a change. Not only were the Jews adopting the ethical and creative elements of the Czech nation, but the Czech people too were beginning to accept many of the contributions of the ethics and the spirit of Judaism, of which the most important element was the Golden Rule, to treat your neighbor kindly and compassionately, with an open heart and a receptive mind.

That estate on the mountain was comparable to a castle to me, a fortress overlooking the Elbe Valley and the city of Schönpriesen. My grandparents modestly referred to it as the *buckl*, the "hump." On a clear day, you could see the peaks of the big and little Milleschauer, part of the foothills of the Ertzgebirge, the Ore Mountains. Across the bridge from the city of Aussig, high above the valley on a black basalt mountain, stood the medieval fortress of Schreckenstein, appropriately named and loosely translated as "Fear or Terror Rock."

Around the year 1200, so the tale is told, pirates conquered and occupied that fortress. The pirates captured and robbed the merchant ships coming around the bend of the Elbe River by hurling large rocks at the vessels, stealing their cargo, and killing most of the members of the crew. We visited that ruin several times. I used to have nightmares about the abyss of the *Hungerturm*, the dungeon, at least ten meters deep, where the pirates literally threw the prisoners and left them there to die in agony.

Across from the castle, on the other side of the Elbe river, stood a flat-top granite mountain called Marienberg. Legends tell that on that plateau there lived under the roots of the oak trees little men, called *Heinzelmanchen*, busy little imps who planned on eventually rescuing the prisoners in the dungeon of the fortress by digging a tunnel under the Elbe river.

So together, my working-class grandparents and their three beautiful daughters, Gertrude, Minkl, and Ernestine, moved up, elevated—"made *Aliyah*" (after a fashion, although it usually means "move to Israel")—far above the smog, the fog, of the city of Schönpriesen, and the milieu—the local colors of the Jewish quarters—not just geographically, but spiritually as well.

Our Tate painstakingly dug a well with the aid of dynamite, ten meters deep into the sandstone rock, and when the cold water sprung forth after they attached a pump, the family was jubilant. I should mention that while Tate was digging that well or building the retaining walls in the garden—monumental tasks—the family had to fetch water in pails at the bottom of the hill at the Brunl, a spring gushing cold water out of the rocks. The unpaved road leading to the house was steep, rocky, and muddy on rainy days, but my grandmother seldom complained, and in this case, she may not have had another choice. The family needed water to drink and cook with, and for the animals as well. Besides, going back to biblical days, weren't the women always the water carriers at the well for their husbands, their guests, and their animals? The most well-known couples were Zipora and Moshe, Rachel and Jacob, Rebekkah and Eliezer—servant of Abraham who was tasked with finding a suitable wife for Abraham's son Isaak. From my grandparents' elevated property on Cherry Hill, you could see, in the valley, Count Serbenski's castle, the sugar factory, and in the distance near the river, the Jewish quarter.

I was fascinated by that cavity that my Tate dug, and I vividly remember looking into the chasm of the well, which was covered only by a round slab of boards. Every now and then, I would drop a small stone into it, just to see and hear how long it would take to reach the water below.

Anton Jacob and Auguste "Mindl" Knobloch Phillip,
Leah's grandparents. Leah's mother, Gertrude,
Tante Minkl, and Tante Erna, ages 5, 4, and 1.

My grandfather built terraces on the hilly plot of land with the
support of fieldstones to keep the soil from eroding. He planted six
plum trees, four pear trees, and two apple trees. Two black cherry
trees already made their home there. Black and red currant bushes,

called *ribisl*, and gooseberries were also planted. Tate had an herb garden that smelled so delicious, especially the marjoram that Mama put in her potato and vegetable soups and gravies.

Some of the most fascinating creatures on the mountain were the red flying squirrels with huge bushy tails, gliding from branch to branch, tree to tree, their webbed forelegs serving as wings. They were shy, and their slight bodies without their fur were not much bigger around than a pencil. Unlike their American cousins, who were city dwellers, they were cunning, clever and bold, and resourceful rodents.

I remember in utter amazement the carrots, strawberries, potatoes, onions, tomatoes, garlic, celery, horseradish, kohlrabi, rhubarb, and cucumbers that my grandparents planted and harvested. Mama made the best half-sour pickles in the world! How did they make time for all these tasks, all that drudgery?

Beside attending to their immense garden that required countless hours of physical labor, my grandfather was employed in the laboratory of the *Chemische Fabrik*, the chemical factory, in Nestowitz, a neighboring town. They produced cleaning products of all sorts, laundry detergents, soda, hand soaps, shampoos, etc.

My Tate was a member of *Hevra Kadisha*, the Burial Brotherhood that prepared Jewish bodies for burial in accord with Orthodox rules. I remember some experiences he encountered that gave me nightmares. That organization was founded centuries before by Rabbi Loew. As well, Tate belonged to the *Bund*, the Jewish workers association.

I vividly remember an incident when I was about seven years old. One afternoon my tired Tate sent me to the bowling alley in the valley with a milk can in my hand to purchase for him a draft beer. I successfully purchased the beer and proceeded to ascend the mountain to my grandparents' home, swinging the milk can back and forth, around and around over my shoulders, and when I finally arrived and proudly handed my Tate the milk can, all that was left was a small amount of foam. Tate, who was not a patient man and well known for his quick temper, just stood there staring at me angrily for a few minutes, no doubt very disappointed. I still feel bad for him to this day, not to have delivered safely a well-deserved treat after a hard day's work.

My grandparents, to my delight, kept chickens, ducks, and geese. Their flock of geese was more vigilant than any watchdog. The geese frightened everyone. For a long time, I was the only child and grand-child. The geese pinched me several times, especially when I teased them with a long stick. Oh, and let's not forget the two goats that supplied the family with milk. Yuck! The goats' milk I had to drink had a nauseating taste, but the cheese that Mama made from the milk was really good. Densely textured, it was quite tasty with veggies and vinaigrette dressing. No electrical service led to the house. Their sources of light were petroleum lamps, and their sources of heat were wood- and coal-burning stoves.

I remember that our dog Vera and the gander of the goose flock often accompanied my grandfather halfway over the mountain on his daily trip into the next valley of Nestowitz until he chased them home. I wish I had a picture of that precious scene.

Tate and Mama were of the opinion that they were autonomous and independent, having provided for themselves and their children all the essential food sources for survival. But man does not live by bread alone. Had they provided their children enough stimulation and spirituality for a belief in a higher power? Of course they did.

At night, one couldn't miss the splendor that God created and couldn't stop fantasizing about the vast universe that was so strikingly visible from that summit. My mother and her sisters imagined those billions of luminous objects to be the souls of our ancestors, observing them, guarding them.

They named their plot of land *Amselgrund*, "Blackbird Estate," after the red-winged blackbirds that competed with them as if they were the rightful owners of the sand-pine-covered domain. It was a constant struggle to keep them from eating the ripening fruits at harvest time. Our Tate in his ingenuity led a long wire from the house to the cherry trees, and on that wire he hung glass bottles close to each other. Every time someone stepped outside the house or heard a noisy flock approaching, they pulled on the wire, and the clanking noise chased away droves of the black pests. He also hung bottles on the branches of the trees, and whenever a breeze would blow, the glass bottles chimed. I remember well those delightful, magical sounds.

My grandparents certainly were a perfect example of Romanticism blended with Realism, which was already inherent in the genes of the

Bohemian Jew. Mama and Tate were not in the ranks of the elite upper class, nor among the famous artists, poets, or musicians, but they were self-taught, skilled architects, builders, landscapers, and virtuosos in their own right. Incidentally, my Mama taught herself to play the zither. Those enchanting, sweet notes of that instrument still are a pleasing memory.

Menschlichkeit, decency, integrity, modesty, and education of the heart were the top values in our family. Dietary laws were observed, but Shabbat services were seldom attended after they moved away from the Ghetto. In fact, my mother writes in her notes that as she grew older, Mama and Tate became more and more involved in political issues. Secret meetings were held at their house with Tate's friends from the Bund, the Jewish Workers' Association, who were all members of the Socialist Party, and my mother was sternly told to never talk about them in school. "*Zei still, mach deine Augen zu und schlaf ein.*" "Be quiet, close your eyes, and go to sleep." As a child, when you are told—as she was—never to speak of conversations you hear in your own home, you tend to think that all is not well, that perhaps the members are doing something wrong, and of course that would affect your self-esteem. Mutti said that her low self-esteem stemmed from those experiences. She heard many political discussions in the German, Czech, and Yiddish language. I am not an expert, but could these experiences have been the underlying cause of the clinical depression she suffered later in life?

I had similar experiences, and the words "*Sei still*" were repeated countless times throughout my childhood. I became extremely shy and, yes, I had low self-esteem because of these occurrences. Thank God I am not tormented by depression!

Chapter 5
My Mother's Early Days

My mother, whom I always called Mutti and will continue to do so in these memories, writes of an experience that really distressed her as a child and far into adulthood. She attended public school where Catechism was taught once a week. She was the only pupil who was sent out of the room to sit outside the door in the cold, unheated hallway during Catholic religious instructions, for being "confessionless." I believe this means "without religious affiliation." "But am I not Jewish?" she said to herself. Lise Haudig and the Teichmann girls stayed for the Catechism class, and they were Jewish.

Was there anti-Semitism in the newly established government of Czechoslovakia? Perhaps. But Tomas Masaryk, the new leader and founder of the republic, often spoke encouraging words and always acted as an outspoken friend of Jewry. In fact, he counted many Jews as his best friends. Jews were active in the government; they were headmasters and teachers in public schools and professors in Czech and German universities. It does sound as if the Jews were making progress. Or were they?

Going back to my mother's school experiences, there was no doubt in her mind that her own mother, our Mama, my grandmother, would have been more than willing to be taken into the fold of a Jewish community. She was our matriarch, in a world of our own when she lit the Shabbat candles, regal, thoughtful, and deliberate. She lived the Torah by the observance of the *Shabbath* or *Shabbat*, the Sabbath, by her countless deeds of *chesed*, kindness.

So what made my grandfather think that being affiliated with the Jewish community was unimportant? Let's find out what could have influenced his attitude, his thoughts.

It is conceivable that my grandfather, who belonged to the Socialist party, though he never had the time to be active in it, was influenced by their doctrine as many of his fellow workers were, Jewish and non-Jewish. In common with their comrades, the only spiritual home to which they owed allegiance was the Socialist movement. Perhaps that theory appealed to him. Realism was in vogue.

It may also be possible that his apprehensions were inherent. Underlying fear and paranoia could have been lurking in his subconscious. In his grandmother's time, under the Austro-Hungarian Empire, even though Kaiser Franz Joseph, who ruled for almost two-thirds of a century, was popular with his people and tolerated the Jews in his empire, the Catholic church was very influential in the provinces of Bohemia and Moravia. People of Jewish origin, whose faith was still looked at as a handicap, had almost all converted to Christianity if they chose to be active in governmental agencies, civil service, judiciary posts, and teaching positions, etc.

To give a few examples, the world-famous Jewish composer Gustav Mahler, in order to secure a position at the Kaiser's court in Vienna, had to convert to Catholicism. Heinrich Heine, a German Jewish poet, saw baptism merely as the ticket of admission to European culture, and the German Jewish Liberal Party admired Emperor Franz Joseph as the champion of Jewish civil rights. The Jews named their children after him and celebrated his birthday every August.

Perhaps that period was not very menacing to the Jewish people, but it certainly was debilitating and didn't encourage religious education or development. But then, the Jews for thousands of years had to blend the never-ending struggle of adaptation with the ever-changing regimes and their rulers. Somehow they always prevailed.

Of course, I am only speculating about my grandfather's individuality and judging him a bit harshly, I suppose. He was a product of the assimilation and the Socialist movement and sort of an enigma to most of us. He was steadfast, loyal, honest, unpretentious, proud, and stubborn. I am convinced that few people were his confidants. To me, he was like a legend. I loved and admired him.

Back to the three Phillip girls. The sisters were different as day and night. Sara, my mother, was well-behaved in school and at home, but she was painfully shy. On her report cards, all subjects were labeled as "*sehr gut*, very good," but when she had to recite a poem, she simply couldn't do it. Tante Minkl always helped Mama with household chores and cooking, sort of a "goody goody," whatever that means.

Our Tante Erna, the youngest, was also the boldest. She didn't have a shy bone in her body, Mutti said. She would go from store to store singing or whistling songs when she was as young as four, and because the storekeepers found her to be irresistibly adorable, they showered her with marzipan and chocolates. But perhaps, on the other hand, this was because she wouldn't leave until they did.

When she was ten years old, she enrolled herself in the *Tschechische Schule*, the Czech school, because she was expelled by the principal of the German school for misbehavior. She supposedly sat in a tall wastebasket she couldn't get out of, rolling and rolling around in it and causing a scene. She had the whole class of fifty students laughing and shouting. Fortunately, by attending the Czech school, she became fluent in the Czech language, which in the coming years proved to be a necessity.

Mutti said she admired both of her sisters, but had to admit that secretly she was envious of them. Her sister Minkl could practically faint on demand and therefore got all of the attention, and Erna, the youngest, was the most popular kid in town.

Erna learned to swim at an early age and caused a scene when she tried to swim across the Elbe River. The river was deep and treacherous, and the traffic of coal barges and merchant ships was constant. Huge dredging machines regularly went up and down the river to deepen the broad stream, and then they deposited the sludge and stones on the banks. Onkel Hans came running from his nearby tailor shop and helped to rescue that little imp.

The Elbe was a constant source of entertainment for me as well when I was a child. The most exciting times were in the spring when all the children gathered to observe the *Eisgang*, the ice drift. Huge chunks of ice on the flooded, swollen river came rushing downward at tremendous speed from the mountainous terrain, carrying with them anything that was in their way. Sheds, doghouses, trees, boats, even small homes at times. One spring, a partially submerged barn had on its roof a cow standing on wobbly legs. I can still see it, poor creature, no doubt eventually drowned.

When the family moved up on the mountain, the seclusion and solitude of that precious piece of land eventually delighted my mother. It was in that atmosphere that she developed a flair for the arts. She was especially gifted in sketching expressive faces of individuals, as well as sketching animals and flowers.

Her teachers strongly advised that she further develop her skills in the fields of ceramic painting or fashion design. When she was fourteen years old, she did indeed enter a training program in Dresden, Germany, where they created the famous hand-painted Meisen china. But to her dismay, she developed allergies to the various paint supplies. How sad that she couldn't continue to cultivate the unique gift that God endowed her with.

However, my Mutti proved that it is never too late, and at the ripe old age of eighty, with charcoal pencils, she began sketching many scenes of Jewish principles and was honored at an Art Show at Sinai Synagogue, in South Bend, Indiana.

After her early disappointment over the discontinued instructions in perfecting her art techniques, my grandparents suggested to Mutti that she should consider taking up the occupation of seamstress, and for a couple of years, she was an apprentice for my Onkel Hans, Mama's half-brother. Onkel Hans had a successful *Schneidergeschaft*, tailor shop, and there was no doubt that he would be a good teacher. Tante Minkl was employed as a nanny at the Steiner home, which was fortunate because the unemployment rate in the years of 1930-31 was very high and poverty began to reign all over the country of Czechoslovakia.

Luckily, the Mars family went on to enlarge the *Zuckerfabrik*, the sugar factory, in our town of Schönpriesen, which would give many young people the opportunity for full-time employment. At that facility, they made brown sugar from the sugar beets grown in the area, and from that extraction they produced many by-products, such as molasses, all sorts of fruit syrups, marzipan, fondant, hard candies, bonbons, and candy bars. They also processed grain into alcohol and this, combined with their sugar products, turned out some of the finest liqueurs in the world. My Tate's favorite was the *sveska konjak*, the plum brandy.

My mother told of the fairness of the Mars family to their employees. Mutti's friends, among them Lise Haudek, were employed at the *Zuckerfabrik*, which was not far from the tailor shop. The girls had heard of a woman named Mietze who served good soups at her home for only fifty *hellers*, pennies. So during the *Mittagstunde*, the noon hour, Mutti was invited to eat there. And that is where she met my Papa, her soul mate.

My father, Julius Peska, in Augsburg,
West Germany, in 1948.

Chapter 6
My Papa

PAPA, MY DEAR FATHER, when meeting my Mutti at Mietze's soup kitchen, was at that time unemployed, but he did give private lessons in stenography, typewriting, and art. In fact, he was sort of famous in the neighborhood for sketching and painting beautiful portraits. Well, that was right up my mother's alley! She was extremely inspired and made arrangements to take art lessons.

My grandfather, my Tate, on the other hand, was not at all impressed. He told his daughter that she was to "Stay away from that old, unemployed Czech by the name of Julius Peska!" But Papa, smitten with my beautiful green-eyed mother, didn't give up so easily. He was an *edler Mensch*, which is a compliment of the highest order, meaning he was gentle, refined, humble, and had sweetness of character. And let me elaborate on the significance of what a "Mensch" is.

As I grew up, I heard it said many times, "Be a Mensch, behave like a Mensch." To be a Mensch has nothing to do with success, wealth, or status. A lawyer can be a blockhead, a doctor a klutz, and a professor a fool. The key to being a real Mensch is nothing less than character, dignity, and a sense of responsibility. Many a poor man, many an ignorant man, can be a Mensch.

Papa wanted to follow all the acceptable rules of the *Shidduch*, the meeting process for finding a mate. You had to follow certain rules until you were married, such as having a chaperone at meetings between the couple. My Papa was thirty years old at the time, and Mutti was seventeen. Our Tate made sure that there was always a chaperone present, and generally, this was my grandmother's youngest brother, Hans.

My great-uncle Hans was a *schneider,* a tailor by profession, as I mentioned before. He was a 5'3" little *packl* of dynamite with a sharp tongue, but with a delightful sense of humor, an enchanting entertainer at all times. For instance, he could surprisingly produce a piece of candy from behind his ear or a flower at the end of his sleeve. I was told he, as well, was an expert at card tricks. One of his cutest *Vitzes,* jokes, in my opinion, was sitting cross-legged on top of the cutting table to be closer to the light bulb hanging from the top of the ceiling, when he would say: *"Drei mol hob ich obgeschnitten, und ist noch zu kurz!"* "Three times I cut it off, and it's still too short!" What is he talking about, I thought to myself, as a five-year-old. He was a *Kibitzer,* a kidder, and more than a *shtickl,* a little, crazy. Now, of course, I think he was adorable.

Back to Mutti and Papa. My grandfather soon discovered that my father could be trusted. Papa had an uncanny ability for making friends, and, after a year, my grandfather gave them his blessings to marry. They, Mutti and Papa, decided to have a civil service at the *Standestamt,* the City Hall, much to Mama's and the Babbi's misgivings. Mutti emphasized that she married my Papa, who was a double amputee, out of respect and admiration, and because of the extraordinarily fine human being that he was.

Sadly, my Papa wrote most of his memoirs in "short shorthand," in the style that journalists use. Not only can I not translate them, but in addition, many of them were damaged by dampness and mold when my husband put several boxes in storage, and they were later discarded by a well-meaning family member. I know that he intended to rewrite them one day, but unfortunately, his enthusiasm and his health unexpectedly failed. Many facts and precious remembrances are gone forever. I found a few pages written in longhand addressed to me, written by my Papa in German script rather than shorthand. They were insightful, poetic, and full of good judgment. And of course, there were Mutti's manuscripts, when she recorded all that she could recall, describing the unbelievably tragic occurrences that befell my Papa's family, and a short version of my Papa's life.

My Papa's Early Days

Papa was born in 1902 in Schönpriesen, Austria-Hungary, to a Jewish mother, Molly Richter. Molly came from an upper middle class family. The family boasted about the grandfathers and great-grandfathers having come from a long line of magistrates in the small villages across the river Elbe. Molly's mother's maiden name was Shandy. My mother's notes reveal little information about the extended family, and most of my Papa's notes, as I said, were written in shorthand. One of the rabbis indicated that perhaps back in the Middle Ages

Ferdinant, Papa's brother, died of malaria.

Rudi, Papa's brother, died
of typhoid fever at age 14.

when names were chosen for the Jews by fanatic Germans or by members of the Roman Catholic Church, the name "Shandy" could have originally been *"Schande"* which means "shame" in German and Yiddish, so perhaps the family chose to modify it by adding the "y" at the end. And then again it could be of Irish heritage. Perhaps she was one of the "black Irish." I choose not to know because my family tree is eccentric enough.

Molly's family were the owners of a thriving business in the field of cobblestone road maintenance and bridge construction. Despite her parents' objections, Molly, my grandmother, married the son of a farmer from the interior of the country in a small village near Prague that I cannot find on the map of the Czech Republic. Joseph Peska was of Czech descent, without any religious affiliation. Molly was a very beloved daughter, but the Richter family did not approve of her choice of mate.

Because her husband Joseph was not Jewish and came from a lowly peasant village, Molly was discriminated against by the whole family. Her brother Karel married within the Jewish faith. Eventually, Karel inherited the prosperous business and all the properties of the Richter family. My mother states in her memoirs that she finds it very hard to forgive the members of that family for making life so difficult for Molly and her descendants, who after all were Jewish!

The marriage of Molly and Joseph was a happy one and produced five sons and one daughter. When in 1914 World War I broke out, the three oldest sons, Ferdinant, Frantisec, and Zeph, had to serve as soldiers under the Kaiser of the Austro-Hungarian monarchy. Julius, Margit, and Rudi were still living at home.

The path through life was to become a long, hard journey for the Peska family. Papa's youngest brother Rudi, who was only fourteen

Margit, Papa's sister, died from complications
of Spanish influenza at age 24.

years of age, drank water from a brook while out hiking with a group
of friends. Two of the boys were infected with head and stomach ty-
phus and died under agonizing pain. Rudi was one of them. Papa said,
"Rudi's last request was for my Papa, his brother, to tickle his feet!"
Nebach. How sad.

In 1917, just before the war ended, his brother Ferdinant was already on his way home on a ship near Italy, when he was struck with
an attack of malarial fever that he contracted in the wretched conditions on the island of Madagascar. He died on the ship and was buried
at sea. Tragic! My Papa's beautiful sister Margit resembled his mother.

Dark hair and dark eyes—a beautiful young woman. Shortly before she was to get married to a boy from a fine family, she was exposed to the Spanish influenza that ravished Europe at that time.

After a short, devastating illness, Margit died of pneumonia. That influenza epidemic raged across the globe, causing fifty million or more deaths worldwide. It took more lives than even World War I. It created devastation among the civilian populations and the military. It was catastrophic!

My grandmother Molly, God rest her soul, was by now inconsolable beyond description. Where were the members of the Richter family? Had they no *Rachmonos*, no compassion? Every time I think of the unfathomable pain and anguish she must have endured, I am sad. *Boruch Hashem,* God bless, she still had her Julius, my Papa, who was a kind and caring young man. But unfortunately, the *tsoris,* the trouble, does not end here. My Papa, while playing *Fussball*, soccer, seriously injured his knee. The doctor advised that the knee should be put in a cast.

There was at the time a severe shortage of both food and fuel, such as coal, and people stood in line for hours just to get a loaf of bread or a sack of potatoes and a heavy bucket of coal. These staples were distributed by the Czechoslovakian government for the needy, impoverished population. And that's what my Papa went out for on our behalf—my Papa, cast and all, on a brutally cold winter day. In those days insulated boots were not available. Papa said they used to wrap newspapers over their socks for insulation before putting on their boots. Well, apparently that was not sufficient, being exposed as they were to the sub-freezing temperatures. I guess his circulation was impaired by the tight-fitting cast, and in addition, he probably was undernourished and obviously exhausted. Papa whimpered and cried for I don't know how many days or weeks, and finally the doctor removed the cast from his knee. It was too late. Gangrene had started to eat away the flesh on his limbs. How did this happen so quickly?

Finally, the Richter family came to the rescue! Papa was driven to Prague by his Onkel Karel, my grandmother Molly's brother, where a team of doctors amputated his left leg up to the thigh and the right foot up to the heel. At age fifteen, he was the victim of an incompetent doctor who robbed him of his limbs, deprived him of his youth and of a normal existence. Mutti also said that shortly after the operation he went into heart failure, or perhaps it was kidney failure, or maybe both. His slight body retained fluid, and he swelled up like a balloon.

A concerned neighbor contacted a "healer" from Budaweh, a small village across the river Elbe. She examined him and said: "Give Julius *Hagebutten* tea three times a day." Hagebutten are the rosehips, the fruit of the wild roses that grew at the edge of the fields. Rosehips are rich in potassium, vitamin C, and antioxidants, and they are as well a diuretic. That eccentric lady obviously knew her profession well, because miraculously Papa eventually recovered. A "healer" is not necessarily an eccentric old lady, but a person learned either by folklore or experience in how to regenerate and rejuvenate a body back to health with the aid and treatments of well-known teas such as chamomile for relaxation and stomach aches, or apple cider vinegar to help digest food because it is full of enzymes, contains large amounts of potassium, and purifies water, or rosehips, the above-mentioned source of vitamin C. Today we call the "healers" nutritionists, who recommend preventative methods to stay healthy rather than relying on medical miracles.

In his notes, Papa mentions that his dear mother was by now just a mere shadow and cried herself to sleep every night. Her heart ached for her Julius. How was he to survive and make a career for himself? Could he ever find a woman who would marry him?

One day, by the light of a candle, she descended the basement steps, perhaps to fetch a bucket of coal, lost her balance, and tumbled to the bottom. For days she *schlepped* herself around in pain. My grandfather contacted Molly's brother Karel. He immediately drove her to Aussig an der Elbe, and then upon the physician's recommendation took her to Prague, where they performed some kind of surgery.

Molly died during an invasive procedure. Her brother buried her in Prague, and we have yet to find out where they laid her to rest. She was 53 years old when she died. Papa mourned the death of and honored his dear mother's memory all his life. I believe, among many other issues, she obviously died of heartache.

Feats of Self-Reliance

Now the disabled young man was alone with his father. His two older brothers married and moved out of town. Papa was not entitled to a pension, as he was not injured in the war and he was too proud and too embarrassed to apply for aid from the government or Jewish welfare organizations, and one must also keep in mind that he was barely fifteen years old, did not have a Jewish education, and therefore was not aware of the affiliated organizations. So he schlepped himself around on a pair of crutches for many months until, at last, he did get a prosthesis.

Papa's notes do not express one word of self-pity. Papa's actions speak louder than his words. His heavy prosthesis at times was not comfortable and was often painful, yet he seldom complained. With the help of his father, whom we called "Votta," and Onkel Karel, he purchased books and began a home study program in typing, stenography, bookkeeping, mathematics, journalism, philosophy, sociology, and Czech and German literature. A few years later he passed his tests at the University of Leipzig, in Germany, which must have been between the years of 1922 and 1924. Papa was no more than twenty-two years old. How unbelievably courageous and focused he was!

During his self-improvement period, he also needed to support himself. Of course, his father, who was employed as a locksmith for the city of Krasne Bresno, did all that he possibly could to make life easier for his son Julius, who wanted to save money to acquire a "state of the art" prosthesis to feel like a whole human being again.

Because Papa had always been artistically inclined, his good friend Lucac Novak suggested that he inquire into painting scenery for the theater in Usti nad Labem. The director of the theater at that time was Franz Allers. Jewish, he was born in Karlsberg, Bohemia, and in later years in America became the leading conductor of Rogers and Hammerstein's Broadway play *My Fair Lady*. It sure is a small Jewish world!

Papa's physical limitations made it difficult for him to climb ladders, which sometimes was necessary in order to paint the picturesque backgrounds. Much to his embarrassment, his co-workers were always willing to help lift him up and down the scaffolds. Later, when he perfected his drawing techniques, he graduated to painting portraits and designing posters on billboards.

Among his many friends were artists, writers, philosophers, and poets. They often engaged in long discussions in our apartment about the state of the economy, the rising unemployment, the poverty rate, anti-Semitism, and social unrest with all of its possible causes. His friends introduced him to the famous book, *Das Kapital*, whose author was Karl Marx, an unobservant Jew, who among other issues believed that "the individual, not God, is the highest being in the universe."

Papa was inspired and filled with enthusiasm about the International Workers Association, dedicated to improving the life of the working classes. The idea of unionizing industries, which could include profit sharing for the proletariat, got him all fired up. However, Papa was a pacifist, and Marx's idea of a social revolution to achieve those lofty goals did not appeal to him at all.

More to his liking was Tomas Masaryk's social philosophy of "Menschlichkeit and Realism." "Do not adhere to phrases and words, but to deeds, because only then can you improve matters, and whatever cause you serve, keep to Reality." This was one of many of Masaryk's well-known quotations. Perhaps he found that profound thought in the Torah, the *Chumash*. "Deed outweighs potential!"

Masaryk was educated at the universities of Prague, Vienna, and Leipzig. He began his career in 1891 in the Austro-Hungarian government, where he fought for the rights of the Slavonic, Hungarian, and Ruthenian minority groups, which included the more religious Jewish population. Masaryk was always a supporter of Jewry. Worthy of mentioning as well would be that he traveled to America to study our constitution and returned home with an American wife.

He had many serious challenges to conquer throughout his life, trying to satisfy the missions and visions of the seventeen nationalities in the Austro-Hungarian Empire, as well as in his newly established Social Republic of Czechoslovakia, where he was elected to be president in 1918.

After the disintegration of the Hapsburg monarchy in 1918, the migration of Jews from the villages and small towns to the large cities like Prague, Pilsen, and Aussig was a serious problem. In addition, Jews from Russia and the Ukraine, who were victims of pogroms and political persecution, came streaming into Bohemia, Moravia, and Silesia. Most of them were able to improve their social and economic status, but the ones that did not became a burden on the Czechoslovakian Republic and the Jewish welfare system.

Papa said that on the street where he and my grandfather lived, many transient beggars slept in the doorways at night, *schnorring*,

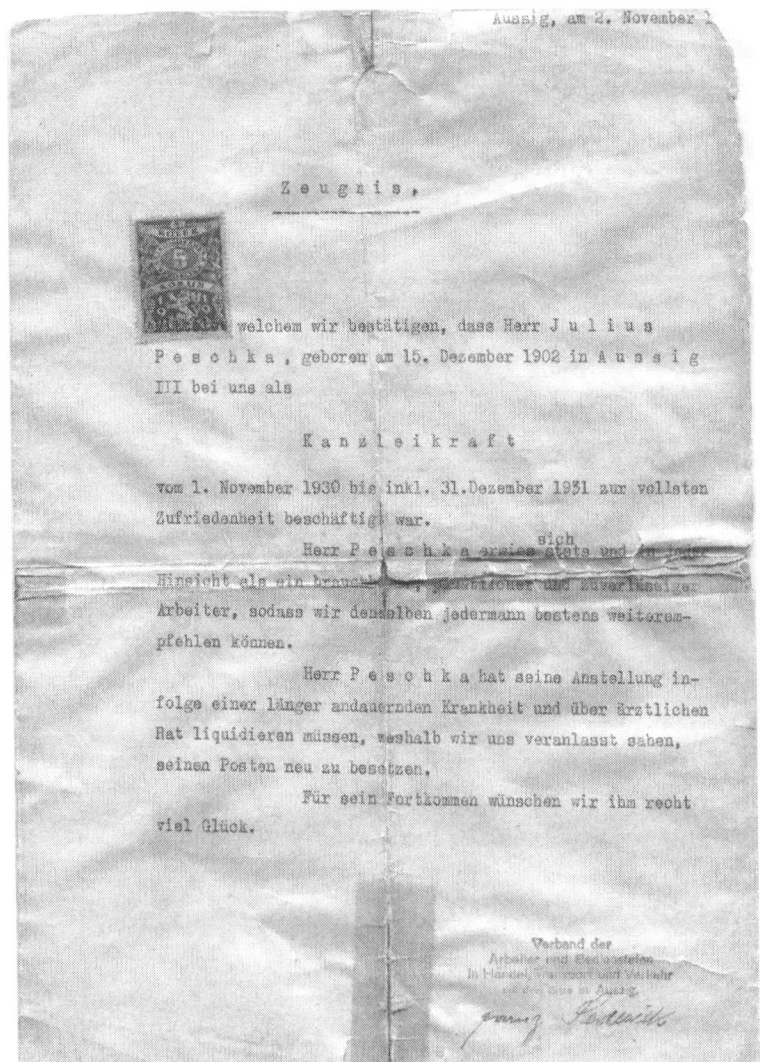

begging, in the streets by day. Thousands of young men roamed the streets, without a profession, without work, and without even a purpose. In their battle for survival, the only alternative to acquiring a productive way of life was to break with their old principles.

Now fragile with age, these identity papers provided proof of employment for Julius Peska through the 1920s and 1930s.

Amtsstelle B
der
Allgemeinen Pensionsanstalt
in Prag II., Rašinovo nábřeží 60.

Fernsprecher Nr. 424-5-1.

Bescheid
über das Erlöschen der Versicherungspflicht.

My Papa's Multifaceted Passions

As in the case of most countries, analysts and journalists played an important role in the financial policies of their nation. And when the opportunity arose to work with prominent journalists, such as Gustav Stern and Robert Korb, Papa was very inspired.

The soil in Czechoslovakia was fertile for a shift to the Left! The Jewish youth groups established a Left Center and a Socialist Zionist Group. These organizations formed a special brand of Liberalism that was adopted by the majority of the Jewish population in Bohemia, Moravia, Silesia, and Slovakia. The Zionist movement chose Liberalism as well, but according to Papa, some Jews opposed Zionism and Jewish Nationalism and declared themselves to be Czechs or Germans, not only by citizenship but also by nationality, and Jews by religion only. I believe that my Papa was one of those Jews who were proud to be *Bohmisch*, Bohemian. Please note that my Papa's political views and philosophies are not necessarily mine. I am only trying to analyze, understand, and perhaps even justify his political ideologies by considering the impoverished and tragic circumstances of his childhood.

In one of Papa's articles, he criticized a few members of the Czechoslovakian parliament for not giving enough support to the workers' unions. For these daring accusations and for rabble-rousing at city parks and market places, he was imprisoned for a six months term in the medieval penitentiary of Bankrats, in Prague. Rats, roaches, and bed bugs thrived in that primitive isolation cell.

Demonstrations were held on his behalf by his friends and eventually by the members of the *Liga der Menschenrechte*, the "League of Human Rights," whose headquarters at that time was located in Lucerne, Switzerland.

Because of the support of that organization, he was released from Bankrats after a three-month term. My Papa had lost so much weight during his imprisonment under those wretched conditions that his prostheses no longer fit. Mutti told me that his friends carried him to the train station on their shoulders.

The Communist Party offered my Papa a stay at a rehabilitation center on the island of Krim, today better known as Crimea, which at that time was considered the "Riviera" of the Russian Empire. As well, they invited him for a visit to the Kremlin. Votta, Papa's father, didn't trust the Russian regime and convinced Papa to resign from the party. So Papa left the Communist Party and joined the Social Democratic Party. Because Papa had a nervous breakdown after the ordeal of imprisonment, he was sent to a convalescent home by the Czechoslovakian government, to Reichenberg in the Giant Mountains in Silesia.

There he regained some of his strength and vigor by learning the art of metaphysics. Papa tried to explain that concept to me many times. Metaphysics is a science that investigates and studies the ultimate nature and relation of fundamental conceptions, such as space, time, matter, force, life, mind, will, cause, motion, etc. Unfortunately, I didn't pursue learning the amazing concept of metaphysics.

Sadly, after Papa's mother's death, there was little Jewish observance in the home. But Papa was no stranger to the never-ending struggle of Jewish survival. He and his friends did not only discuss politics, they also had many heated discussions about the many diverse theories of religion, one of which was "Religion is the opiate of the masses." Did Karl Marx forget that for thousands of years, while those around us were wallowing in the darkness of stupefied ignorance, captivated by countless superstitions, the Jews were pursuing the path of knowledge and learning with unswerving loyalty, which they demonstrated in the practice of their faith?

Papa always also weighed and pondered the concept of who was to be the rightful owner of the "Jewish Spirit." The Orthodox Jewry, of course, was first in line. They are the guarantors of Jewish survival. They are able to withstand the harshness of even the most cruel and inhospitable physical environments, such as had the Jewish population in the Subcarpathian regions. Yet, the role of Orthodoxy is by no means confined to preserving only its past heritage. The dream of a messianic era certainly is oriented towards the future.

Needless to say, the Jewish Assimilation movement was the complete opposite of Orthodoxy. It represents the Jew who is ready and willing to blend with all cultural values, German, Czech, French, Hungarian, or American, whatever the case may be. He is open to the ethnic customs and ideals of any host nation with whom he happens to live. He may in the process be spiritually elevated, or he could be emotionally depleted.

Papa didn't compare himself to either one, neither the Orthodox Jew nor the assimilated Jew. He was on a mission of his own, which was to secure his immediate needs and that of his impoverished comrades. Unhampered by anti-Semitism, he had lofty ideas about the future and unswerving faith in the Czechoslovakian government and its people.

Zionism was a topic that my father examined thoroughly as well. Its roots go back to the sixth century BCE, when Jeremiah and other prophets implanted the idea of the hope of returning to Palestine amongst their people living in exile. Often through the centuries, self-proclaimed messiahs tried to organize mass movements but failed. So, Zionism did not come to its fruition until a new movement began under the influence of *Haskala*, Enlightenment.

The movement was started by the German Jewish philosopher Moses Mendelsohn in the eighteenth century. Jews tended to become more worldly and less religious. They were inclined to look at action rather than prayer for the solution of their problems. Theodore Herzl organized such a movement at the end of the nineteenth century. In 1907 Bohemian Zionists established their own weekly newspaper in the German language called *Die Selbstwehr, Self Defense*. It became the foremost periodical in Czechoslovakia. The representative from our district of Usti na Labem was Hugo Stern, and according to my grandfather's recollection, he believed that Mr. Stern was the father or an uncle of Gustav Stern, who in later years was an associate journalist who worked side by side with my Papa.

Chaim Weizmann, first president of Israel, joined the Zionist movement around 1904. He was educated at universities in Germany and Switzerland and was a delegate of numerous congresses of the World Zionist Organizations. In 1917, the British government issued the celebrated Balfour Declaration, which eventually led toward the establishment of a national home for the Jewish people.

The adventurous and daring proposal of building a Jewish home in Palestine crossed Papa's mind only fleetingly. "Who needs a cripple without legs?" he said. "I can't even get out of my own way at times." And besides that, he was a pacifist and despised war. War robbed him of two of his brothers. War invites poverty and pestilence, and he had seen his share. In retrospect, however, he later regrettably realized that his strong convictions of equality and humanism could have been of benefit in helping to establish the kibbutzim and motives that were built on those values, and on the ideas and ideals of Socialism.

Papa had explored all avenues and came to the conclusion that joining the Socialist party was the right decision for him. He was to become an "edel Communist." I have no clue what that label signifies. All I know is that my Papa was an honorable and indeed an "edler Mensch." With his academic qualifications, it was soon realized that he had the capability for leadership, which he never sought but was always thrust upon him. Wherever he went, there soon gathered around him a circle of friends and scholars. People who came in contact with him ended by making him their confidant and seeking his advice. He was a master of the Czech language as well

Papa Julius, age 20, assistant editor of two newspapers,
Der Tag *and* Die Internationale, *in Bohemia, 1922.*

as of the German tongue and could converse with people from any Slavic-speaking country.

The Socialist Party offered my father a position at two Socialist newspapers as a *Hilfsredakteur*, an associate editor. He eventually published his own editorials, critiques, and commentaries for the tabloids *Die Internationale* and *Der Tag*. Among his friends and co-workers were Robert Karp and Gustav Stern. Papa was proud to work beside these two men he so admired and respected. They were full of confidence and optimism, convinced that their cause would usher in a new, almost messianic era, bringing about liberation from servitude, discrimination, aggression, corruption, and lay to rest envy and greed.

Just recently I have re-read Rabbi Wein's book *Triumph of Survival*. Rabbi Wein, whom I respect very much, is, in my opinion, the authority on Jewish history and his opinions are widely spread. He states with legitimate reasons, I suppose, that the "non-Jewish Jews" were members and in many cases leaders of the Socialist party, held blind hatred against their own traditions, their own people, especially against those of the ultra-Orthodox movements. I had never perceived the Socialist cause in that light, had never looked at it from that perspective, but I do think that "hatred" is too strong of a word and certainly doesn't apply in each case. My father simply didn't have that negative character trait in his gene pool.

Undeniably, my Papa's motivation was to find a path out of the canyons of dire poverty that proletarians, the working classes, were imprisoned in for so many years under Kaiser Franz Joseph's imperialistic system. I agree with Rabbi Wein's belief that Socialism, because it discourages religious affiliation, promotes assimilation. The fruits of that doctrine were very bitter ones in the decades to come.

Chapter 7
My Early Days

I WAS BORN IN AUSSIG, CZECHOSLOVAKIA, weighing barely four kilos, in 1933, the fateful year that Adolf Hitler became Chancellor of the German Reich. My mother, my Mutti, said I looked like a monkey, with long black hair growing all over most of my skinny body, but both of my grandfathers and my Papa thought I was beautiful! I was named Liane Leah Peska. Most family members called me Lia and the only one that I remember pronouncing Leah in *Hebräisch*, Hebrew, was my great-grandmother Shoshanah.

My mother had a very difficult delivery. She suffered from eclampsia cramps and was admitted to the hospital in Aussig with life-threatening seizures. This condition can develop in pregnant women who have a disposition for hypertension. The medical staff in the 1930s may not have been aware of that important analysis. Mutti was warned never to become pregnant again.

Unfortunately, Hashem had many more challenges ahead for the Peska family. In November of 1932, much of the European population was in a panic and held their breath as the election in Germany approached. The results were inconclusive, but after negotiations, Nazi leader Adolf Hitler became Chancellor in 1933, edging out adversaries, including the Communists, in an emergency cabinet dominated by Nazis and their partners. Times were very tense indeed!

The Communists started milling in the streets of Berlin and other metropolitan cities, and violence erupted. The country was at the brink of civil war in the years to come. Because of these critical occurrences, Hitler went on to make elimination of the Communists one of his key goals.

The global spotlight was now drawn to Czechoslovakia, a faraway place that people in London and in Washington had never visited or even knew how to spell. The country was famous for the province of Bohemia, a land of magic, marionettes, and the golden city of Prague, the Maharal, the Golem of Prague, Jon Huss, and perhaps Pilsner and Budweiser beer.

In 1933, Papa was very concerned. He knew that Hitler was a dangerous creature, but just how perilous, how power-hungry and bloodthirsty he would turn out to be, no one knew at that time. Certainly, there were enough signs, enough hints that his targets were not only the Communists and Social Democrats. In fact, foremost of all, the Jews were to be his main prey.

Hitler's stated opinion was that the aim of Communism was not to create a dictatorship for the proletariat, but a dictatorship for the Jews. My Papa was a Jew, a former member of the Communist party, and now a member of the Social Democratic party. This realization made Papa very anxious and disturbed. And soon thereafter his fears became reality.

In his frenzy, Hitler arrested fifteen thousand of his opponents in Poland alone, and because there was nowhere to send them, Heinrich Himmler, the Nazi police commissioner, came up with the idea of the concentration camp. Mostly Communists, Social Democrats, Romani, and of course Jews, were the first inmates, accused of trying to crush the New Germany.

Adolf Hitler also announced his program of the perfection of the Aryan Race, weeding out Germans who were less than perfect, and we don't have to use too much imagination in assuming that the Jews, the subhumans, the *oysvorf*, the trash of society, as Hitler viewed them, were the first on his list to be eliminated. I am not sure where I read all the information about Hitler's program of "perfecting the Aryan race." My parents, when attending a movie, said that you had to watch the current newsreels as a preview. In America, we watch endless commercials and reviews of films to come. One of these films, *The Eternal Jew* (1940), showed the Jews running around like rats under the Nazi occupation. In comparing the Jews to rats, the film, which was shown to the German public and to the world, suggested that those pests could only be eliminated by extermination.

We wondered how any observer, let alone the tough-minded Winston Churchill, could write that those who met Hitler found him a "highly competent, cool, well-informed functionary" with a "disarming smile" and "subtle personal magentism." So, the world lived on hopes that the worst was over. But that was not to be the case.

In 1934, Papa was hospitalized three times. The diagnosis was stomach ulcers, which were treated at that time by drinking heavy cream to promote healing. *Nu?* When he developed *Gelbsucht*, hepatitis, and had several attacks of excruciating pain, the doctors operated and discovered that he had thirteen gallstones, which resulted in the removal of his gall bladder. His recovery was slow and painful.

Papa hadn't even recovered yet when an old friend, Willi Stolle, came for a visit accompanied by Papa's cousin Franz, Onkel Karel's son. Franz inherited the road construction business after his father Karel's untimely death. Franz obviously was an opportunist or perhaps just a good businessman, because in order to secure the road contracts that were now in danger of being scarfed up prematurely by the *Reichsdeutsche*, Germans from the Empire who invaded the Sudetenland. Franz married the Burgermeister's daughter. But here comes the icing on the cake: Franz's new father-in-law was a Fascist, forerunners of the Neo-Nazis.

Because of the connection to the Fascist regime, better known as the Nazi Party, Franz and the Burgermeister had access to incriminating information about my Papa. Mutti suspected that Franz had no other choice but to join the Nazi party himself. And perhaps not. Keep in mind that my Mutti always had a long list of conspiracy theories. Franz may have entered that marriage just for the sake of retaining a successful business, but who am I to judge? The survival instinct is very powerful.

Franz told my Papa that he was on "the number one list of enemies of the Reich" in our district, and reminded him of his past daring political affiliations. Papa's cousin Franz said, "Julius, we will lay our hands in the fire for you if you promise to do the same for us some day. We will erase your name from the list to whitewash your past, change birth records to keep the entire family safe, and tell the authorities that you were only an idealist and could never be a threat to any government. But Julius, you must promise to keep your mouth shut about your *meshugene*, your crazy, radical ideas of Equality and Liberalism. And, '*Gott im Himmel*,' please burn Lenin's picture hanging on your wall, along with the book on your bookshelf titled *Imperialism*." Needless to say, Papa was fearful for the safety of his family and was agreeable to just about anything that Franz suggested.

During that period in my parents' life, I began to take my first steps. After observing my progress for a few weeks, they decided that I was not walking normally. I walked like a duck, from side to side. Mutti was hysterical. "*Votta im Himmel*, she may have to join the circus someday," was my Onkel Hans's opinion. One doctor said, "Your daughter has a hip deformity, but it's not so bad, and she may outgrow it." Another one explained that it was only the one hipbone that was severely deformed and so I would only limp on one side. Nu! Well! Would you be satisfied with an answer like that?

Fortunately, I had responsible parents. They took me to an orthopedist in Prague by the name of Dr. Glasser. He strongly advised that I be put in a body cast for at least one year, off and on. He explained that the procedure would at least partially correct the abnormal bone formation and may avoid scoliosis in the years to come.

Papa was still too sick to work full time, so Mutti found a position at the Jewish firm Eisenman. They made cellophane covers for wine bottles. Mr. and Mrs. Eisenman, their son, and a widowed sister with two children escaped to the interior of Czechoslovakia before the Nazi occupation to find a safer location. Mutti as well worked for a medical firm that made cough medicine. The name of the firm was Robitussin, believe it or not! They no doubt migrated to America before the war.

Votta, my grandfather Peska, was to be my caregiver while my Mutti worked. He spoke the German language only sparingly but made up for it by laughing a lot and by being patient and loving.

At age two, I was exposed to the chicken pox while I was still in the body cast and of course, most of the pox developed underneath the plaster. Some of the pox became severely infected, and I had to be taken back to Prague, where they removed my cast, only to replace it again with a new one two weeks later. My parents cried for me, but I, on the other hand, have no recollection of any discomfort. All I remember is the love and special attention I received from all the members of my family.

Life on the Streets in Our City

My grandparents, Mama and Tate, used to race up the stairs to our third-floor apartment in competition to be the first ones to hug me. Tante Erna promised to buy me a tricycle and Tante Minkl brought me *Kirschknödel*, cherry dumplings, my favorite. Onkel Hans, famous for his magical tricks, came often and amused me by making objects disappear, only to find them again under his *cepice*, his hat. They referred to me as *"Goldene Madi,"* golden girl. Because

Pappa, Mutti, and Leah in an extra-wide carriage because she was in a body cast due to a bone deformity, in 1935.

my legs had to be spread widely to help my hipbone to reform, Votta, my grandfather purchased an extra-wide carriage, in which he took me for long walks along the banks of the Elbe River and to the *Stadt* parks, the city parks, for concerts. Every park in the city had concerts that were government supported city festivals. My guess is that several dozen citizens attended, sitting on benches or on the lawns among the wildflowers, listening to the famous Strauss waltzes or marches. I remember those times with love in my heart for my Czech grandfather.

In 1935, Tomas Masaryk resigned from the presidency of Czechoslovakia and Dr. Benes was to become the new leader of the Republic. Even though Papa vowed not to be obsessed by the *"Schweinspolitik,"* the political status quo in Germany, one couldn't ignore the dangers of the escalating anti-Jewish measures of the Hitler regime.

But he was temporarily encouraged by our new leader, Dr. Benes, who seemed not to be intimidated by Hitler's terrorism. In one of his radio addresses, he said, and I quote from his carefully recorded words: "We in the Czechoslovakian Republic will direct our state in the future as in the past in accordance with the principles of Liberalism and Humanism. We will not betray our whole thinking."

It was Dr. Benes's belief that in Czechoslovakia all seventeen nationalities must be fully recognized and protected. "No Jew in our country could be persecuted," he said, "as long as his allegiance to our state remains beyond doubt!" What a courageous statement that was! Shortly after that, Dr. Goldstein, a member of the Czech parliament, praised the government as still being an island of democracy in Europe. We would soon find out what Hitler's response was to all those humane and praiseworthy declarations.

Fortunately, Papa had regained his stamina. Mr. Gittel, Papa's supervisor at the Welfare Office, was pleased to have him back full time. He put Papa in charge of placing orphans into suitable homes. Mutti was obsessed with everyone's health. She supervised Papa's diet conscientiously and force-fed me butter and eggs, oatmeal, and biscuit omelets called *"Kaiserschmarrn,"* Kaiser Franz Joseph's favorite dessert. Mutti observed every step I made after the cast was removed and seldom let me out of her sight.

Mutti, Pappa, and Leah
with a bear, in 1935.

Even though I was doted upon, I led a lonely existence as an only child and felt like the solitary, feeble little bell that I heard now and then in the distance from the church tower. My Mutti occasionally had bouts of depression, and during those periods, I spent many hours sitting on the broad windowsill in our third-story city apartment, watching smoke rising from the stacks of the *Zuckerfabrik*.

On sunny days the smoke curled straight upward into the horizon where it eventually disappeared. My Mama, my grandmother, read to me year after year the story of the Exodus, which always both fascinated and frightened me. So, when on cloudy days the smoke and the smog lingered and spread its dark shadows over the rooftops and filled the Elbe Valley much like a picture of the ninth plague, the plague of darkness, with the promise of sinister dark seasons ahead.

Dread filled me with visions of crying children searching for their parents in the dark, narrow streets of Egyptian cities. Between the years of 1933 and 1948, darkness was creeping into the intellect of men. It robbed them of basic human values and decencies. The light that illuminates one's soul had dimmed.

The aroma from the sugar factory still fills my nostrils from time to time. Not too unpleasant, much like sourdough bread baking in the ovens of Tante Erna's bakery, and similar to the odors of the ethanol plant in South Bend, Indiana, built to process corn into fuel.

I watched the pigeons, the doves, crows, and ravens, often perched right on the broad window ledge in front of me. The ravens always startled me. They glared at me with red eyes and were known to steal shiny objects, such as jewelry if you carelessly left it lying in the windowsills. I did not try to tame the dozens of shy birds that landed around me. We had no screens on the windows because there were no mosquitos in Czechoslovakia at that time and with my enterprising nature, it's a miracle that I didn't fall off that ledge. Flies, however, made their way into our third-floor apartment only to get stuck on the sticky flypapers hanging from every ceiling. I always felt bad for the flies when watching them struggle to get free.

The house across the street where my Papa's father lived had as tenants a stork family living in a huge nest on top of the red tiled roof. After vacationing in sunny Africa for the winter, the storks returned to our Bohemian town in the spring, year after year. The male could balance on one leg for hours, standing guard and defending, if necessary, the female sitting on her precious eggs. I read that storks mate for life. How's that for loyalty! Such a thing among humans is almost unheard of in today's society!

The Mischke family lived in the apartment below my Grandfather Peska. Years later, my parents told me they were of Jewish descent. Their only daughter, Traudl, was occasionally allowed to play with me. Sadly, she died of an infestation of tapeworms at age nine. That makes me shudder even to this day. Mommy told me that those parasites could be caused by eating un-kosher meat, such as pork.

When I review my notes, I can hardly believe the bizarre, horrific, and suspiciously medieval diseases and unfortunate circumstances that our family, friends, and neighbors had to endure.

As I mentioned before, my Mutti suffered from clinical depression, which was diagnosed after the war. I spent a lot of my days sitting on the broad windowsill, longingly observing the world below. I can see the children skipping rope and playing ball on the street where you could only see an occasional horse and wagon. An automobile was an unusual sight. The vendors were out on the sidewalks early in the morning, selling local fruits and vegetables. There were men on street corners sharpening knives and scissors, and the cobblers repaired your shoes right on the spot. The vendors announced their presence as soon as daylight broke by simply shouting or singing in a loud, clear voice that they were open for business. Their carts were not horse-drawn, but had two large wheels and two long handles and were pushed by the vendors. Some of the salesmen juggled the fruit to get some added attention from the public.

I was fascinated by the *Rauchfangkehrers*, the chimney sweeps who were employed by the city to clean everyone's smokestacks on a bi-monthly basis. That service, I'm sure, helped avoid many house fires. The chimney sweeps were a picture right out of the Middle Ages, hopping from roof to roof, dressed in black uniforms and black top hats. Various different-sized, large, round brushes on long wires were wound around and carried over their shoulders. Their faces and, I am sure, their lungs were just as black. The whiteness of their eyes and that of their teeth, in contrast, was so exaggerated that it scared many a child, including me.

Popek's candy store was on the same block as our apartment building. They had the best gummy worms and also a product of the *Zuckerfabrik* called *Prause*. This was a yellow powder that you had to add to water. It then hissed and fizzed and foamed, but sadly never tasted as good as the fascinating process promised.

I can hear the music of the *Ringelspiel*, the merry-go-round, part of the amusement area set up yearly by a group of Romani and sponsored by the Mars family, who were the owners of the sugar factory. "*Frauen sind zum küssen da, freilich ja, freilich ja . . .* Women are here to be kissed, yes indeed, yes indeed," the ridiculous song was playing over and over on that merry-go-round. To this day, I can hear the music of the Ringelschpiel when I close my eyes. It was so generous of the Mars family to offer the public such a treat!

My Papa's return from his office was always eagerly looked forward to. Mutti and I would often wait for him to arrive on the *Electrische*, an electrically operated trolley. My Papa was always dressed elegantly in a suit, a white shirt, a vest and bow tie as well as a hat. I would jump up and down when the dinging of the bell announced his arrival. Papa was at all times ready to converse with me, patiently answering dozens of questions that plagued me during the day. "How do you make glass? Where does the sun go when it disappears at night? Does God live in a castle above the clouds?"

One afternoon, when Papa returned from his office, he said, "Hop on the trolley, we're going back to Aussig. There is a Moor, a Moroccan, at the market place you must see!" And, lo and behold! There sat cross-legged on a carpet on the ground an impressive-looking Afrikaner, with a huge blue and white turban wrapped around his head. For quite a while he remained motionless in a trance-like meditation.

Slowly he began playing a delirious, charismatic melody on a wooden flute. All of a sudden, out of a large, round basket appeared an awesome cobra, apparently captivated and charmed by the mystical notes coming from the instrument, and that snake, after hypnotically performing an exotic belly dance, proceeded to curl up again at the bottom of the basket. Papa was right. That fascinating sight was indeed worth seeing.

Despite the fact that my Papa was a double amputee, he and I, with the aid of his cane, wandered in the *Stadtpark* along the gurgling brook to the end of the path and on to the waterfall. Only the most aromatic violets grew in the *Leinischen Höhle*. The scent of those violets filled the whole valley. The park was named after the village Leinisch, that perched on the hill above the waterfall. And a Hoehle suggests a hollow, a cavity. The village of Leinisch is no longer on the map of the Czech Republic either because most of the small farmers that were Jewish, Czech, or German left the area, or because the Czech government changed the German-sounding names into the Czech language.

There in the park, Papa made little waterwheels out of sticks, propped them up between two rocks, and the flow of the rushing water in the brook sent them into motion. I can still remember exactly how he constructed them from willow branches. The waterfall, at the end of

Tante Erna won a beauty contest
at Krasne Bresno, in 1935.

the path leading into the hollow, was a sight to see. A wide stream of water came gushing over the cliff and then turned into a gurgling brook. I think, with a little imagination, a reader can picture a little wheel hanging between two rocks, being set into motion by the rushing water. Sorry, I'm not talented enough to draw a picture of that scene. I only paint walls despite the fact that both of my parents were artists. I must say, the formative years, especially the first five years of my life, were full of adventure and happiness, thanks to my loving family, despite my occasional feelings of loneliness and insecurity.

I remember my Tate and I, with the aid of his self-constructed wooden sled, ascending a steep hill by the name of "*Drei Kreuzen.*" On that pinnacle, perhaps the town official, or someone else had erected three huge crosses. From there, Tate and I skillfully guided that sled through the deep snow, around hairpin curves, past the Brunl, past Tante Erna's bakery, almost all the way into the city of Schönpriesen. The cold wind and the snow blowing in our face. Delicious!

Even in the bitterly cold winters, our city streets served as a source of entertainment. Because we didn't have snow plows, and the shop keepers only cleared the sidewalks, the snow accumulated on the streets and soon the snow turned into a thick layer of ice, and because traffic was almost nonexistent, it seldom presented a danger to the children who used the streets as an ice-skating rink.

I was perhaps seven years old when my Tata sent me to the bowling alley in the valley with an empty milk can to fetch him a liter of beer. I paid for the beer and started my journey back to my grandparents' home, swinging the milk can, which contained the cold beer back and forth, around and around over my shoulders and when I proudly handed the milk can to Tate, all there was left was a small amount of foam at the bottom of the can. My Tate, who was not a patient man and well known for his quick temper, just stood there staring at me for a long time, his face turning red. I feel bad for him to this day for not delivering his well-deserved treat after a long day's work.

I guess in my memories, and in occasional dreams, I still see the world through child-like eyes. I have yearned to walk on the familiar paths again, sit on the bench under the linden tree at the foot of my grandparents' mountain estate. In the spring the scent of the linden blossoms filled the air, as did the blooming acacia trees ascending the mountain. We have linden and acacia trees in America, but I have never detected a scent from the blossoms. Could it be that the soil in the Czech Republic had different properties? What did the blossoms smell like? An overwhelming scent of jasmine!

Near the bench was a spring, the Brunl, that gushed cold water from out of the rocks. On a hook fastened to a rock hung a tin cup for the thirsty, weary passer-by. Perhaps I should treasure those fleeting moments rather than be disillusioned by reality. Maybe the Bohemian Jew was too much of a romantic and not enough of a realist and too attached to the soil. Surely those precious, memorable landmarks will have disappeared by now.

And with whom would or could I share my memories? There is no one left. My mother was my only link to the past in the last thirty years, and I could never convince her to go back to visit our place of birth. She said she was not courageous enough to face the bitter-sweet memories without our Papa, her soul mate.

My Mama and Tate, My Maternal Grandparents

In 1937, I was four years old, always looking forward to spending occasional weekends with my grandparents on the *Amselgrund*, the "Blackbird Estate." My grandmother, whom everyone called Mama, was the light of my life. A no-nonsense lady, she was forever involved with some project, and each task took on importance, whether it was weeding the garden or feeding the chickens, the ducks, and the geese. As I said, the flock of geese was more vicious than any watchdog. They announced your arrival when you were only half way up the mountain.

Mama made challah without a recipe, without measuring cups, and the coal stove had to be just the right temperature for baking. She made Gefilte Fish from scratch, by grinding the carp that my Tate caught in the Elbe River. She could stretch chicken paprikash to feed a multitude of relatives and friends. The rule was, ten times more.

My grandfather, my Tata, *shocheted*, slaughtered his own animals in accordance with kosher law, by cutting their throat with a razor-sharp knife. To make sure that the knife had a keen edge, he would use a *Streifriemen*, a leather strap, to sharpen it. He then let the animal bleed until he was certain that all life had ceased. I believe that by today's rabbinical standards, without a rabbi's supervision, that meat would not be considered Kosher. The steady repetitive motion of the razor knife on the leather strop had a sort-of-a singing sound. And when the sharpness of the knife was tested easily on my grandfather's thumbnail, then he was convinced that he could slice the jugular vein of the intended animal.

My Mutti tells me that my Mama was always present when Tate gutted his animals. She was like a surgeon, examining very meticulously the lungs, the liver, the kidneys, and the stomach to make certain that there were no impurities or no signs of disease present, which would have made the animals un-kosher? I believe they discarded the heart, and then the meat was soaked in salt water to help draw out the blood. The chicken fat was rendered and, to my recollection, always tasted much better to me than the meat. We would toast a slice of rye bread on the *Platte*, the top of the cast iron stove, rub it with a clove of garlic and then smear on the chicken fat. Yum!

When strawberries were in season, Mama made marmalade, and when the cherries were ripe, she made *Kirschknödel* dumplings out of yeast dough, and served them with melted butter and sprinkled with sugar and some sort of crumbled farmers cheese. I helped pick the cherries, and also gooseberries and currants. I would climb to the highest branches of the cherry trees to get the juiciest cherries.

Once in a while, Mama took me into the forest to pick wild red and black raspberries. Hazelnut bushes grew wild at the edge of the forest and the fields, and black walnut trees supplied us with walnuts and chestnut trees with chestnuts. My grandmother's crunchy chopped liver and golden chicken soup was to be remembered as well. When my Tate started his journey into the next valley, our dog Vera and the gander of the flock of geese followed him to work until he chased them back home. I wish someone could recreate that scene.

On his way to and from the *Chemische*, the chemical laboratory where my grandfather was employed, Tate had to cross the *Krebsberg*, the Crab Mountain, on which in the evening musicians practiced their instruments. Apparently, there was an ordinance in the city of Krasne Bresno against excessive noise.

Thus, the Krebsberg became the location for amateurs to blast off their distressing, disharmonious tones on their trumpets and trombones. Family and friends sat in my grandparents' grape-vine-covered gazebo many evenings listening to the magic notes of our great masters. However, by the end of the summer-fall season, the quality of the notes of the musicians had developed into inspirational, ecstatic trumpet concertos by Beethoven, Haydn, Mozart, and other great masters. This entertained us many evenings when I was at my

The author at age 6.

grandparents' home. The tunes of the lively recitals echoed across the valley and were appreciated by avid, grateful listeners.

I remember my Tate telling me about his father, who apparently was absent a great deal of the time because he was a captain of a ship. There are so many questions that I didn't ask when my loved ones were still on this earth. Was he a captain of an ocean liner, or perhaps of a tour ship or merchant ship?

His mother, my paternal great grandmother, whom everyone referred to as the *"Alte,"* the old one, used to rock me back and forth on her lap, using he long skirt as a swing murmuring, over and over

"Mein Hoitele, mein Hoitele." I have no idea what that meant. Is it possible that I've retained these memories since infancy?

For hours I would watch the chameleons and the salamanders skillfully dart in and out of the rocks, and I would observe the snails very cautiously slide their heads out of their round shells, looking at the world with curious eyes sitting on top of two little antennae-like feelers. The ants in our part of the world resided in high rises. They lived and toiled in huge mounds, expertly built of pine needles, leaves, and soil. Their work ethic set a model to be embraced. One of my hobbies was making hair bands and hair crowns out of wildflowers, cleverly weaving them together.

This fairy tale existence during my formative years molded me into an incurable romantic, a dreamer, a *Luftkopf*, an airhead. Not that I had an empty head, for learning was Papa's priority. I was able to read long before I attended school, and my math aptitude was at college level when at age fourteen I attended high school in West Germany, as a result of Papa's and Onkel Joseph's homeschooling program. Homeschooling was constructed in a very calm, patient manner whenever the time or circumstances allowed. Never demanding, only motivating. When, for instance, we were in the hop fields, we spoke about philosophical ancient events or historical incidents or misfortunes. We also learned and practiced over and over math calculations in our head, like, for instance, 357 times 143. It sure made you concentrate! But we will continue this self-study and self-critique elsewhere in my memoir, as I am just beginning to know myself through the process of reliving the past.

We visited a synagogue in Aussig only a few times. Recollections of the rabbi and the congregants are fuzzy, but the *Tallisim*, the prayer shawls that the men wore, were impressive and memorable to me. I imagined Moses high on the mountain wearing a similar shawl. The *davening*, praying, and the chanting were intimidating and unfortunately foreign to me. But I vividly recall the famous coffee house "Savoi" and the French and Austrian pastries piled high with *Sahne*—whipped cream—that Mutti fed to me by the spoons full because she thought I was much too skinny. "Look, Julius, Leah's ribs are showing again!" she would say to my Papa.

Seeking Dangerous Adventures with the Romani

Because an overanxious mother overprotected me, I had tremendous pent-up energy and had developed an adventurous streak. Since age five, my goal was to explore the forest behind the local castle inhabited by Count Serbenski. I had a picture taken by my cousin Ewald in 2005 from the summit of my grandparents' estate. It clearly showed the castle as well as the woods and the clearing where the Romani might have set up their tents. I wish I could share it with you. I'm sure the castle to this day has been well maintained. I don't remember more than two violin players, probably because there were only one or two families that camped in the clearing. Cimbaloms were used by the women that danced to the rhythm of the lively tunes.

Count Serbenski had an only son, who had attended school with Papa. He was a fragile, sickly boy and sadly was eventually confined to a wheelchair for the rest of his life. The rumor was that the affliction was caused by generations of inbreeding. Just gossip, I presume.

There were in those years about 450,000 Romani who roamed around Czechoslovakia in colorfully painted wagons. Most of them spoke Czech and German as well as Romani, and some of them were indistinguishable from the Czech population. Count Serbenski gave permission to some of them to set up camp at a clearing in his forest right behind his castle.

By trade, they were peddlers, blacksmiths, skillful craftsmen of copper and brass, and of course accomplished circus performers and animal trainers, as well as gifted violin players. Stories circulated that there were also some who were thieves or prostitutes, who stole the chickens out of your back yard and lived in squalor with ten to twelve children in one room or one wagon. They preferred superstition to modern life.

One day, when Mutti was occupied conversing with a group of neighbors, my friend Olli Frieser and I headed for the castle, a short distance from our apartment. We climbed the ancient stone wall and made our way through the thickets until we reached a clearing where some Romani had set up a stage for an upcoming performance.

On a thick wire, that was fastened between two trees about three feet off the ground, several girls ranging in ages from three to ten were practicing for their high wire acts. A baby, not much older than ten months, was balancing on the palm of her father's hand. I admired them and thought they were wise to train them at an early age.

Someone was always practicing haunting, passionate tunes on the violin as I sat under the trees listening to them. Those intense, stirring melodies are embedded in my memory.

A group of boys juggled balls and bottles, throwing them high into the air and then skillfully catching them. Dogs, cats, and chickens were running around, and several women were speaking excitedly and very loudly in a strange exotic language. I presume that it was Romany. Had it been a Slavic or German language, I might have been able to follow part of their conversation.

I was fascinated by their way of life, which appealed to me, and because of my enterprising nature, it would have been quite easy for this band of nomads to kidnap me. They were said to engage in *verschleppen*, kidnapping children.

Imagine my mother's *Schreck*, fear and worry, when she couldn't find me for several hours. Needless to say, I was placed under house arrest for quite some time, but still I managed to observe that group of captivating individuals again and again, wishing that I could move about without restrictions with that transient race. Little did I know that self-fulfilling prophecy was to come true all too soon.

Childhood diseases were very common at that time, and for some reason, I was always their target. I was exposed to scarlet fever when I was five years old. The condition was serious enough, but within two weeks I had recovered, only to find out that my Papa was now breaking out in a suspicious red rash all over his body. His eyes were swollen shut, he couldn't swallow and therefore was not able to eat or drink and his fever was off the charts. I am sure quarantine was part of the health laws concerning childhood diseases.

My Papa was always a nervous man, and now this additional impairment undermined his fragile character. He lived in terror of being unable to give his family a happy and comfortable life. Work had now become the sole aim of his existence and left him in an agitated frame of mind.

Assuming that the disease had to run its course, our Tate waited several days, but after realizing in time that Papa's condition was not improving, he took matters into his own hands. He flung Papa over his shoulder and carried him to Dr. Schickl's office, one floor below us in our city apartment. Papa without his prostheses only weighed about seventy pounds. The doctor ordered bed rest. He explained that a severe strep infection might leave scar tissue in the chambers of his heart. He was to be right.

Mutti, during that time, acquired a job at a *Naturheilgeschaft*, a health food store, equipped with vitamins, minerals, and all kinds of natural cures for the common cold and a long list of other ailments. My favorite was the chewable vitamin D tablets called "sunshine pills." Today these products are known as preventative or alternative medicines. The store had a variety of herbal teas and many brochures filled with recipes, one of which my mother made for me at least three times a week, called "*Muesli*," until I was sixty-five years old! Did I ever thank her enough for that labor of unconditional love? I want to share that favorite recipe with my friends and family here in my book.

Muesli recipe

1 cup of old-fashioned raw oats
1 large apple, grated
1 tablespoon of honey
Juice of ½ lemon

Mix all dry ingredients. Grated apple and lemon juice will moisten the raw oats. Nuts can be added.

Yes, Mutti was a smart lady, way ahead of her time. She also experimented with a new and different type of hamburger patty made out of soybeans and herbs, but Papa didn't appreciate it.

Votta, Papa's father, had not been feeling well lately, and he had been unable to care for me, so I occupied myself as best as I could, roaming around in our three-room flat. The large kitchen had a soft sofa in it, and it was always warm and cozy near the stove. Come to think of it, schlepping coal up three floors couldn't have been easy for Mutti and Papa.

I couldn't wait for Papa to come home to check my writing skills and to bombard him with endless questions about the creation of man and the mysteries of the universe. He would tell me about the Jules Verne books that he read, and we would fantasize about what Martian creatures might look like. We spoke about God and the creation of the universe and that of man.

Fear and uncertainty in 1939.

Chapter 8
Times Change

THE YEARS OF 1937-38 brought grave anxieties to Czechoslovakian Jewry. It was by that time clear that Europe was headed for a new and terrible crisis. Within a few years, Hitler had occupied the Rhineland and incorporated Austria into Greater Germany.

So far, the 380,000 Jews still living in Czechoslovakia, not counting the many Jewish refugees who found asylum there, were relatively safe. They had faith in the Czech people and were convinced that they would continue on the path of justice and humanity. But that was wishful thinking.

We knew that Hitler had become more and more daring. "Give us back our colonies and a corridor through Poland to conquer Russia," I remember him screaming at the top of his lungs. Hitler was referring to Prussia, *Preussen*, which was a former German colony under Kaiser Wilhelm. Mutti writes that the Bohemian Germans were becoming very confident that they were going to become the ruling party. They had visions of being *knockers,* big shots, soon. The village idiots walked around with signs that read: "*Heim ins Reich*!" Home to the Empire. Papa and Tate said: "That's impossible, we have never been part of the German Empire or collaborated with them in the past."

A couple of years previously, Hitler had declared several times that he had no interest in the Sudetenland and that it was the last territorial demand he would ever make in Europe. And again, that statement gave us false hope. Unfortunately, Hitler seemed to have changed his mind. He wanted to conquer all of Czechoslovakia, not just the Sudetenland, which included the provinces of Bohemia, Moravia, and Silesia.

We heard of the frightening episodes of *Kristallnacht*, the night of broken glass, when the Nazis shattered windows and looted the stores of the Jewish merchants in Germany, and cruelly attacked countless Jewish-German citizens, in the year of 1938.

Many Jews were now in a frenzy to depart, and those who could not make comprehensive arrangements at least prepared for their children to evacuate to safer locations. That undertaking was called the *"Kindertransport."* Jewish organizations from South Africa and England provided financial aid to help Jewish children emigrate. "Thank God, we don't live in the Reich," my Mutti said, but the close proximity, right over the Ore Mountains of Nazi Germany, was giving her nightmares.

As I stated earlier, we wondered how an intelligent politician like the tough-minded Winston Churchill could state that "Those who met Herr Hitler face to face found him to be a highly competent, cool, well-informed person with an agreeable manner and a disarming smile." So, while the wider world nurtured ill-considered hopes that the worst was over, we Czechs soon found out what Hitler really had in mind.

And then, on September 30, 1938, in the city of Munich, Germany, at a four-power conference, British Prime Minister Chamberlain, Premier Daladier of France, and Premier Mussolini and Adolf Hitler "sold us down the river" by reaching a "peaceful agreement" in handing over Bohemia, Moravia, and Silesia. No Czech representatives were present at that meeting. The entire world decided to sacrifice the Sudetenland to Hitler.

Should Czechs have shown more courage than caution and stood up to a power many times their size? It was not so simple. However, their capitulation led to the Second World War and to the suppression of the Czech nation and its people, which included 380,000 Jews. We lost the freedom we were granted under President Masaryk and President Benes for decades, dispersing people all over the world.

The Czech people are well known for their diplomacy and skills in adaptation, but not for their boldness. If we could repeat Czech history, we could, of course, find desirable as well as apathetic possibilities each time and compare the results.

Der Schwergefaste Entschluss, the Weighty Form of Resolution

And I quote Ludwig van Beethoven, who viewed many of his weighty life decisions as positive. "Only necessity has value and only what is heavy has usefulness," was his opinion. He bore his fate and his impoverished existence, like Atlas carrying the whole world on his shoulders. His point of view was that it was only the negative experiences that teach you lessons and hopefully make you wiser. For instance: From the sounds of his landlord's fists pounding on Ludwig's door to collect the overdue rent, Beethoven composed the brilliant, inspiring notes of the Fifth Symphony. Amazing, what you can accomplish through positive thinking and the determination to improve your way of life.

The Betrayal of Our Neighbors

One night, not long before the *Anschluss*, the Annexation of Austria into the German Reich, my parents turned pale with *Angst*, anxiety, about what they witnessed from their third story window. We later watched the scene from our balcony. "*Shhh, sei still,*" Papa whispered in German. I held my breath. Hundreds of people, the *Sudetendeutschen*, were marching silently, holding lit candles. Papa said the Fascists called it the "*Schweigemarsch,* the march of silence." Mutti was of the opinion that it resembled more a *Totenmarsch*, a death march, out of the darkest medieval period. It was sinister and frightening. Papa called the Sudetendeutschen "*Falsche Hunde,* deceitful dogs!"

For centuries we, the Jews, had a relatively happy friendship with the law-abiding, industrious, easy-going population in our province under the monarchy and the Czechoslovakian Republic. Was it possible that our homeland was going to be overrun by hordes of barbarians betrayed by the majority of the Sudetendeutschen?

71

Would it become too dangerous to stay in our place of residence, or should we move farther inland as some of our friends had? Perhaps we should have applied for a visa, called Tante Fanny in America a long time ago? Did she even have a telephone? We didn't. To be *ehrlich*, to tell the truth, I believe my parents were in denial. A wait and see attitude possessed my family.

In the year of 1938, the *Kaufhaus,* the department store called Yeppa, where Tante Minkl worked as a saleslady, closed its doors. The small medical foundation Robitussin went out of business. We presume that they were able to flee to America, where they obviously promoted their product. We foolishly assumed that these closings were coincidental, but when Strnat's fabric store and Bopek's candy shop closed as well, we knew our days were numbered.

My parents noticed that some of the neighbors were avoiding us now. Some no longer responded to our greetings, especially if we said "*Guten Morgen,*" instead of "*Heil Hitler,*" and sometimes they crossed the street rather than acknowledge us. My Tante Erna, who had a sense of humor, said, "We just couldn't get Hitler's wretched name across our lips," so she suggested that we should raise our hand and say, rather quickly, "*Drei Liter!*" If spoken swiftly, it sounded similar. I was always afraid that people would take notice of these dangerous, nonconforming actions.

My Mutti said, if Papa hadn't been so challenged physically, if we had ample funds to draw from, we would surely not have hesitated in escaping to a safer destination. My grandparents' funds were limited. Most of their money was tied up in the estate on the mountain. The Steiner family left for Hungary, which was relatively safe at that time and when Papa spoke to Dr. Heller in Teplitz-Schönau, even though he had the gravest words of warning for us, he himself stayed on until 1942.

During all this uncertainty and chaos, my grandfather Peska had a heart attack and passed away of pneumonia two weeks later at age seventy-two, may he rest in peace. That was a very sad event. He was a dear, dear man, and I will remember his loving care forever.

In 1939, Hitler's army came toward us as quick as lightning. Within twenty days, and with German efficiency, he had the Sudetenlander under control.

The Annexation of the Sudetenland

I was only six years old, but I remember the invasion clearly. We huddled near the bedroom window, then later went out onto the balcony, from where we could see the *Haupstrasse*, the main street. The silence was chilling and hypnotizing. I was holding my breath, and my knees were shaking. Mutti said I was so upset and uptight that I bit my fingernails until one of them started bleeding. The *Reichsdeutschen* would be here at any moment! "*Schweig, sei still,*" Papa whispered.

The first sounds we heard were the aircraft of the Luftwaffe screaming through the Elbe valley, tipping their wings dangerously toward the city streets. Then we heard the heavy motors of the German vehicles. At least two dozen huge tanks with their machine guns pointed at the public, advanced like giant prehistoric creatures. Hundreds of swastika flags, German steel helmets glistening in the sun, black-booted SS and SA soldiers goose-stepping through the streets of our peaceful town. Unforgettable! More frightening than Darth Vader and the Wicked Witch of the West. Their sheer numbers were intimidating. Orders were shouted through loudspeakers from moving vehicles. I didn't sleep that night and many others to come, reliving those terrifying scenes over and over.

The very next day red flags were flying from almost every house. A bizarre-looking black hooked cross in the middle of a white circle was appropriately named *Hakenkreuz,* hooked cross. To our amazement, one of these flags was blowing in the wind at Adler's drug store, one of our Jewish friends. Herr Adler was Jewish, but not so the mother. She was of German descent and therefore their only son had to serve in the German military.

Posters were nailed to telephone poles and kiosks with long lists of "*verbotene Regeln,*" forbidden orders. Every radio station played German nationalistic marching songs. *Die Fahne hoch, die Reihen fest Geschlossen*, and *Deutschland, Deutschland uber Alles* are still ringing in my ears. Next came the food rationing, curfews, and submissive behavior was essential. It was a strange routine, but strangely enough, within a few weeks it became just that, a routine. "See, Hitler is not so bad. He's just enforcing law and order, creating new jobs," neighbors said. If you kept your head down and your mouth shut, you were able to blend in with the rest of the intimidated population so far.

In 1938, the resignation of Dr. Benes marked the end of the Jewish party as an active entity in the country, and after the Munich agreement, Czechoslovakia could unfortunately not be considered a state of many nationalities. The Jews were helplessly stripped of their rights, and an honorable chapter in the history of Jewish presence in the Diaspora was brought to an end. Many fled, but more than 80,000 Jews were still in Czechoslovakia when the first shot was fired.

Instead of a menorah, we now had a Christmas tree displayed in our window to blend in with the rest of the neighborhood. After the sun set, widows had to be darkened with black shades. Gestapo soldiers were patrolling the streets and sirens were often blaring, at which time we had to descend the stairs to the *Luftschutz Keller*, an air raid shelter. The frightened residents, we among them, sat trembling, wrapped in blankets on the cellar floor, until the sirens indicated that the danger was over. "*Sei still*" always echoed in my mind. Because of the threat of chemical warfare, we wore gas masks that made the experience even more terrifying, because we now resembled creatures from another planet. Those occurrences were always frightful and unforgettable. And every time we heard someone ascending the steps to our apartment, we were holding our breath for fear of having been discovered as Jews.

Following the October 5, 1938, forced resignation of Edvard Beneš, Emil Hácha was elected the new president of the country. Hácha was Catholic by religion and a notable attorney by profession. Hácha, as President, refused to pledge fidelity to Hitler and called the Gestapo "beasts and hyenas." He counted on the valuable advice of his Jewish friend, member of his parliament, and Prime Minister Alois Eliáš. Unfortunately, he did not succeed in protecting his country from the ruthless Gestapo. Summoned to Hitler and Goering in Berlin, he was threatened with the aerial bombardment of Prague and forced to sign a document accepting the incorporation of Bohemia and Moravia into Germany.

Reinhard Heydrich was placed in charge of rounding up and seeking out Jews in the small cities in Czechoslovakia. Many of Hácha's colleagues and friends were arrested, and some were shot. Eliáš was arrested and transferred to the death camps in 1942, just before Heydrich's assassination. Because of the terror campaign started by Heydrich and his butchers, Hácha felt that collaborating with the Nazis was the only way he could help his people and his nation. In 1943, Hácha broke down and was taken to the Pankrác Prison, where he died in 1945. Papa and Tate always spoke of the secret "Hácha army," which became the heart of the Partizan resistance movement, and very successful in protecting the remaining "hidden" Jews in Czechoslovakia. In reviewing Mutti's notes one more time, she mentions that in some cases, especially since Heydrich's assassination by Czech secret agents in 1942, the SS soldiers were intimidated by the Bohemian assimilated masses. The Bohemians tended to be loyal and protective of their friends, regardless of their religion.

Within days of that fateful Munich agreement, Hitler triumphantly arrived in Prague. The Gestapo were spreading throughout the city with long lists in their hands. The colonization of Czechoslovakia was a ruthless exploitation plan of the country's industries and resources, not to mention the brutal oppression of its people.

Principal crops were potatoes, sugar beets, bread grains, flax, tobacco, paprika, poppies, and sunflowers. At the foot of the Ore Mountains, Karlsbad and Marienbad were famous health resorts, known for their natural hot springs, remnants of volcanic action. Skoda automobile works still thrived, and so did Batya shoe factories.

Czechoslovakia was also one of the most important mining countries in Europe, if not the world. The *Ertzgebirge* in Bohemia and the *Riesengebirge* in Moravia and Silesia were rich in coal and iron. Other minerals were graphite, gold, silver, copper, and lead. In the area of Teplitz-Schönau, garnets and other precious stones were extracted from the mountain ranges.

But most important to Hitler were the uranium mines. He needed the uranium for his ultimate goal, the development of nuclear weapons. Hitler had struck it rich! Czechoslovakia was indeed a storehouse of treasures.

German-speaking Jews who stayed in Czechoslovakia were embraced by at least the liberal element of society who, in the tradition of Masaryk, supported human rights and granted Jews citizenship between 1935 and 1937. Until then, Jews in the Bohemian districts were still able to practice their religion, and synagogues, except for the one attack on the Alt-Neu Shul, were undamaged.

Czech Jews were not forced into Ghettos or concentration camps, nor were they required to wear the Yellow Star, until 1942. For most Czechs, the German occupation was annoying, as well as mortifying now that Jews faced discrimination. So, if you kept your mouth shut and your head down, you could go on with your life, or find ways to go into hiding, or somehow leave the country.

So far, so good. No one bothered us. I could hardly wait to get into a real school, but I had to reach my sixth birthday first. Finally, in 1939, I was enrolled in the first grade in public school. Boys and girls were segregated. One side of the ancient building was for girls, the other side for boys. Classes were large, with as many as forty-five to fifty students. Discipline reigned. No talking was allowed. When an adult entered the room, students immediately rose out of respect. We had to show our hands and fingernails daily. If they were not clean or manicured, you were told to kneel on the floor facing the wall for thirty minutes. "*Autsch*, that hurts!" "*Sei still, Leah!*"

You were not allowed to touch anything on your desk while the teacher gave instructions. To ensure that disciplinary measure, we had to clasp our hands behind our backs and hold that position until the teacher gave the signal for us to relax. We were told that position was good for our posture. I was intimidated by the teaching staff and as well by some of the children I walked home with, and I couldn't wait for the day to end. On the way home, at times when the wailing sirens indicated a potential air raid attack, we had to take temporary shelter in a doorway or dive into a ditch next to the road.

Chapter 9
Shocking Nazi Crimes

UNTIL NOW, GERMAN-SPEAKING JEWS who stayed in Czechoslovakia were embraced by at least the liberal elements of society. But in 1941 our family was brought face to face with anti-Semitism. Mama's brother Hans, the little *Schneider*, as I mentioned before, was an outspoken man. He despised the Nazi regime and the *Sudetendeutschen*, calling them *Verräter*, traitors. He was neither an idealist nor a socialist, just a foolish little *Judele* who assumed that he was among friends when he criticized the ruling party.

Several days later, his body was found floating near the buoys on the banks of the Elbe river. A group of fanatic Fascists in a frenzy had beaten him unmercifully. I heard Mama say he was unrecognizable because of the multiple bruises, lacerations, and stab wounds they inflicted on his slight body. I am sure he didn't have a chance to defend himself. No investigation was launched by the authorities about the obvious murder case. "*Oy Tate, Votta im Himmel!* Father in Heaven!" I experienced anxiety attacks and nightmares for many, many days, nights, and years to come any time I let myself think about the tragedy.

Mama was devastated about the tragic death of her young brother. She had warned him many times to keep a low profile. Poor Hansi! So adorable, such a *shlemazel*, an unlucky person.

Onkel Hans Spec, the tailor,
was killed by Nazis in 1941.

Onkel Hans was buried before sundown on the same day, so his soul could ascend speedily to heaven. Mirrors were covered, a custom I didn't then understand. We cover mirrors because we should not be concerned about our appearance during the seven days of mourning while sitting Shiva. We grieved for many days for the unexpected departure of our dear family member.

Mama boarded the train to Teplitz-Schönau where the Babbi lived in the home of a caregiver with several other seniors. To tell her mother the devastating news about her youngest son was one of the hardest duties she ever faced. When she arrived at the facility, the attendant's building was vacant. She went from house to house, asking the neighbors about the senior citizens. Perhaps they were moved to a new location? They supposedly knew nothing, and most of them just shut the door in her face.

What was she to do next? Should she go to see Dr. Heller, a friend of the family? He was not in his office and could not be reached. Mama left a brief note. She couldn't remember the rabbi's name, and then she realized that he might have already relocated to a safer area. Could the Nazis have had something to do with the disappearance of the seniors? Of course! But *Chas v'Sholom*! God forbid!

She should have inquired about Babbi's well-being long before this. After all, Babbi was eighty years old and very fragile.

"We must leave immediately for the utmost last outpost of humanity, the interior of Czechoslovakia or Hungary," she decided. Even under Hitler's occupation, these remained a haven to refugees. Of course, there were some despicable exceptions. "Hitler, that ugly, ugly beast, was destroying our whole world. The *tievel*, the devil, should get him! "*Shhh, sei still, Mama!*

My grandfather—my Tate—several days later was contacted by Dr. Heller about the Babbi. The doctor said that he was told about a few ladies who were taken to Theresienstadt. We heard that this place was a model holding camp where the Jewish population was able to live and work in peace. In fact, we later heard that Jewish musicians gave classical concerts for elite Nazi officers and Jewish children performed German folk dances and theatricals in that camp. That was encouraging news.

However, this propaganda of cleverly fabricated lies was for the world at large, or perhaps even for the German population to see. The truth was that most of the residents lived in squalor, were mistreated, and we now know what Hitler did with the sick and the old.

Bohemian Family Ties

We decided that Tante Erna, who had taken Czech citizenship, was going to be our ticket to safety, "*Im yirtzeh Hashem!* God willing." Her plan was to contact Papa's cousin on his Czech father's side. His name was Stienek Peska. That should be interesting. None of us had ever met him or his family. They lived in a small village near Prague.

I should mention that Tante Erna's husband Joseph Löebl's father was of Jewish descent on the father's side, though Joseph's German mother was not. Jewish heritage passes through the mother down to the children, and therefore Onkel Joseph, as the son of a German mother, had to serve in the German army. Regretfully, he was killed in Kiev, Russia in 1941. I remember how devastated and distraught Tante Erna was as a young widow, but she rose to the occasion, continued to run their bakery single-handedly, with my grandmother's help of course, and made it a very prosperous business.

Traveling to the interior to contact Papa's cousin Stienek was a daring venture, but if anyone could be successful at it, it was Tante Erna, who had *chutzpa* to spare. Incidentally, back in the year of 1936 she had entered a beauty contest and was chosen to be the most talented and most beautiful girl of the district. With her black hair and her dark blue eyes, as well as her winning smile and personality, no one was surprised.

So we were to flee blindly to an unknown destination. Just imagine yourself at the age of eight or nine, in such a vulnerable position! What to take and what to leave behind—a few pictures, some important documents, but nothing too incriminating, of course. Earthly possessions became so irrelevant, so trivial. I can't translate Papa's stenography, and Mutti didn't elaborate on the possibility of acquiring the forged or falsified birth certificates and *Kennkarten*, passports, necessary for survival. Mutti hoped that Onkel Franz and Papa took care of all those details.

I know that Papa was always shuffling documents, for hours studying and inspecting them with magnifying glasses. In later years, my Mutti mentioned that Papa had become an expert at duplicating, copying notary seals and imprints of rubber stamps.

Food, warm clothes, medicines. Almost ready to depart. But, "*Der Mensch denkt und Gott lenkt*. Man proposes and God guides," was a lesson we had to learn over and over again.

The next morning I woke up with a fever and a throat infection. We waited for two days for the condition to improve, but it got increasingly worse. I had been exposed to diphtheria. Mama insisted on bringing me to the mountain, and Tate ran to the city to summon Dr. Schickel, who specialized in childhood diseases. He told my parents that so severe was my case, that the infection in my throat nearly restricted my breathing. When Dr. Schickel fastened the quarantine sign on the door, he saw the Mezuzah, shook his head, and said *"Armes Madl*, poor girl," A Mensch! Wouldn't it have been wise to take the Mezuzah off the door post, Tate, to keep us safe? Or were we safe because of the Mezuzah?

Within a couple of weeks, I recovered but was left with a heart murmur, and because the high fevers reoccurred, I was ultimately diagnosed with rheumatic fever. I remember the arthritic pains in my limbs that were treated with aspirin, hot baths to lessen the pain, and *shmattes*, rags soaked in vinegar water wrapped around my legs to lower my temperature. Not to forget the two tablespoons of honey that were administered and, in addition, a spoon of cod liver oil. Absolutely nauseating stuff! We know now, and they knew then, that both products build immunity and promote healing.

News flash! The German troops paraded through Paris, putting up signs that said, "Germany conquers all fronts!" That was not comforting, and our escape was delayed by my condition.

My mother and I never returned to our city apartment. Papa still went to the office, stayed in the city on weekdays, and made sure to visit us on weekends to check my homework. I followed a study program prepared by him in mathematics and German language, concentrating on *Aufsätze*, essays.

Mr. Gittel, Papa's superior, repeatedly invited Papa and Mutti to private parties, and for weeks they gave justifiable reasons for not attending. My Mutti felt that she was not sophisticated enough to be in the company of city officials, and besides that, she was frightened. How much longer could we hold out? We had been lucky so far, as if someone was watching over us. Was it Hashem, God, or Onkel Franz?

Hitler's mania was far-reaching. He pursued individuals whether they were religious, affiliated, assimilated, atheistic, or not. If they were Jewish, they were a target. Even Gentiles who didn't fit Hitler's fantasy of the *Reine Rasse*, like the Aryan Hero Siegfried with golden hair and *Kornblumen blauen Augen*, cornflower-blue eyes, were pursued. There is no doubt in my mind that Friedrich Nietzsche had to be Hitler's ultimate inspiration. Nietzsche maintained that the virtues of humility, gentleness, patience, and spiritualism were the marks of a slave nature, much like the Jewish race. Nietzsche believed an *Über-mensch*, a superhuman, can only be created by selective breeding and if constantly supplied, can produce a master race, the Germans! He was opposed to the people of mediocrity, who could only achieve a race of inferior men, sub-humans, such as the Jews! *Ich habe mein Sach auf mich gestellt*! was one of Nietzsche's quotations. Roughly translated, this means "I believe only in myself!" Nietzsche's ideas greatly influenced the philosophy and the propaganda of National Socialism in the Third Reich.

On September 6, 1941, the German secret police published an order that all Jews must wear a wide black armband with a six-pointed star and the letters "*Jude*" in the center. I'm sure people tried to avoid obeying the new rule. If you didn't look or dress specifically Jewish, you could possibly get away with it for a while. That proclamation covered the entire Reich, including the Sudeten regions. That year, Germany invaded Russia. At first we believed genuinely that the Germans would finally lose now, but a few days later we felt despair and doubt about the survival of mankind and ourselves, as Hitler's troops confidently and efficiently advanced further into Russia. Well, now the situation became critical.

One evening, when our Tate was crossing the railroad tracks on his way home, he saw in the distance what seemed to be a pile of clothes. As he came closer, he realized it was a human being, a pitiful skeleton of a young girl that my grandfather recognized as being Jewish. He quickly carried her slight body into the underbrush of the nearby forest, where he waited for night to fall.

He lovingly wrapped her in his coat and carried her up the mountain toward the outer rim of the cemetery. He buried her precious body with tears streaming down his face and the Kaddish on his lips. Someone's daughter! What if it had been his! God forbid! He was exposed to enough tragedy and death as a soldier in the First World War to last him a lifetime, but the sight of that violated young girl, mercilessly thrown off the train to or from hell, was heart-wrenching!

The murder of Tate's brother-in-law and the disappearance of his *shvieger*, his mother-in-law, was more than enough. And now this atrocity! Did he thank God a thousand times for keeping us safe up to this time? I'm not sure. More than likely, he questioned God's existence even more at allowing such horrors to happen. "Why did He permit this senseless war with its dreadful human sacrifices? Why doesn't He intervene? *Chazak, Chazak,* run, run, *Ala vanti,* quickly!" was Tate's message now.

The hoped-for sanctuary near Prague was only about seventy-five miles away, but it loomed as an endless, fearful journey. Tante Erna, our guardian angel, had already been in touch with Papa's cousin Stienek. None of us ever had a reason to be in touch before, and whether it was out of loyalty to the far-removed kin or the fact that Tante Erna offered him a generous sum of money he couldn't refuse, he offered us protection for an undisclosed time. They had to have been charitable individuals to put themselves into such extremely dangerous circumstances by extending to us this needed shelter.

Before we left our beautiful town of Schönpriesen, Tate put our wolfhound Vera to sleep. It must have been hard to say good-bye to his loyal friend. Mutti said my Tate cried bitterly.

*Across German-controlled areas of Europe, as the Holocaust
was getting underway, the Nazis required Jews to wear
a yellow star on their outer clothing as a form
of control and psychological torment.*

Chapter 10
To the Interior of Czechoslovakia,
Our New Home

THE WINTER OF 1941-42 was an especially brutal one in Europe. Temperatures seldom reached higher than five to ten degrees below zero, in Celsius. Your nostrils stuck together when stepping outside and the north wind bit at your nose and even when you dressed warmly, your fingertips and toes felt like they were frostbitten.

In the depth of the winter of 1942, Papa's school friend Ladi Klepsch transported the entire family, Mama Tate, Tante Erna, Tante Minkl, with my one-year-old cousin Ewald, Mutti, Papa, and I, in Tante Erna's bakery delivery truck to the remote village near the city of Prague that was to be our new home. We were packed in that un-heated truck like sardines. Despite the short distance to Prague, the journey seemed neverending over the snowpacked, icy roads. There was no snowplow, no salt on the roads. The temperatures were un-believably penetrating, despite the fact that we had the feather beds tucked all around us.

When we approached the border between Sudetenland, now be-longing to the Reich, and Nazi-occupied Bohemia, Ladi and Tante Erna stepped out of the truck and showed the *Kennkarten*, passports, to the SS officers. "*Shhh! Sei still!*" Ladi and Tante Erna conversed and tried to charm them in German and Czech for what seemed for-ever. Our hearts almost stopped when an officer opened the doors, counted our heads, nodded, and left. "Thank you, dear God, the Reich is almost behind us now!" And as a child, I thought, "Are we there yet? I have to go to the bathroom!"

When the Germans wanted to describe boring, backward villages where nothing ever happens, they used the term "*Bohmische Dorfer*, Bohemian villages." Such a rural area did seem to be the perfect niche for us to hide in plain sight with Papa's cousin Stienek Peska. We departed our home town in the dead of winter, so we seldom ventured outside. My Papa's cousin Stienek's last name was Peska as well, the same as ours, and once we arrived at the village we did not wear the armbands, even though we left the city and Sudetenland after the law was passed.

Stienek's father was my grandfather Peska's brother Pavel. He was survived by two sons, Stienek and an older brother. Stienek's wife, Ludmilla, and Papa, the eternal optimist, had not lost faith in the Czech populace. They themselves were victims of oppression under Hitler's tyranny, but there was no looting of Jewish stores there and, but for the one bomb attack on the Alt-Neu Synagogue, no burning of buildings. This was so even though the Nazis did their best to invite anti-Semitism among the Czechs by instituting penalties for Gentiles who associated with Jews. We heard that when some hospital boards and insurance companies began to bar Jewish doctors, many Czechs protested and remained their patients.

During the roughly fifty years of Humanism and Assimilation, with the exception of cities like Prague and Bratislava, most Jews in Czechoslovakia lived in mixed neighborhoods. Christians and Jews went to school together, ate together, fought together, and sometimes even married each other, and when the political atmosphere became critical, almost everyone had a Jewish friend or a Christian relative.

Though as I stated, that involvement was not healthy for a pure, undiluted Jewish family tree, but the truth is that it was just that integration that was central to Jewish survival, as it turned out to be in our case. Because of this lifestyle, thousands of Jews survived in Czechoslovakia and were successful in eventually recapturing our land of Israel.

Still, Papa worried and prepared himself for the worst, although his cousin Franz Richter gave his word to keep "the dogs" from our door. However, Franz himself could be shipped off to the death camps at any time.

Stienek was another cousin who had to prepare himself when asked by his neighbors about the strangers invading their domain. He planned on telling them that his cousin's numerous physical disabilities were the reason why he wanted to live near family members. In addition, Julius had a wife, Gertrude, who suffered from melancholy, a sometimes debilitating condition, and he also had a sickly child who suffered from rheumatic fever. Me! *Nebekh.* ("*Nebekh*" is a Yiddish word meaning "poor thing.")

That sounds fairly convincing and not far from the truth. Tante Minkl, who was such a sweet little lady with an infant son, should not present a problem. As well, we were told that we should all dress like peasants. Sounded like fun to me!

When we arrived after dark, we were shown to a large room over the barn that was attached to Stienek's residence. Stienek only spoke Czech. Straw mattresses made of burlap bags were lying on the floor. A freestanding coal stove was located in the middle of the room. Apparently, Stienek had lit it before we arrived, to heat the drafty chamber. We huddled around it to warm our hands.

We had brought the essentials, feather beds, pillows, hot water bottles, hazelnuts, walnuts, a couple of bags of raw sugar, and rye bread, oh, and mandelbrot (almond bread), and two bottles of Mama's raspberry syrup, which was a comfort in this foreign atmosphere. To this day, the taste of raspberry syrup in a glass of seltzer makes me feel nostalgic. Oh, and let's not forget the cod liver oil, so oily, so slimy, and thank God, we didn't forget the hot water bottles!

Mama, Tate, and Tante Erna drove on to Prague where Tante Erna arranged to stay temporarily with the Fischer family. The Fischer family was somehow related to us through my great-grandmother's second husband, Mr. Osterman. They lived in Josephstadt, Prague in a formerly Jewish area where members of the Fischer family used to be prominent journalists and authors.

I could smell the manure from the animals down below us. I shivered with cold, or perhaps it was fear, and my bones ached. My little cousin Ewald whimpered for hours, so neither one of us slept that night. The only comforting sensation was the smell of the petroleum lamp.

When daylight finally broke, the scene didn't improve. The Middle Mountains and the valleys that made you feel like you were in a nest, or in a cradle, protected on all sides, were gone. The land was flat, covered with ice and snow, and instead of pine and birch trees, the countryside resembled a steppe-like terrain with tall, bare trees off in the distance.

I could hear the mooing of the cows and the clucking of the chickens from below. "Well, there is hope after all," I thought.

As I stated, the village consisted of perhaps one dozen and a half very modest houses, most of them with attached barns or sheds, and in the middle of the marketplace, there was a well with a bucket that you could lower to retrieve the water. What a medieval existence, I thought! At the end of the road, there was a small chapel that rang its feeble bell three times a day.

We were told that the threat of raids by Reinhard Heydrich and his carefully selected entourage of SS butchers was real and frightening. Heydrich was in charge of pursuing and apprehending the Jewish population of Czechoslovakia. Thank God, shortly after Stienek made that statement, Heydrich was assassinated in the city of Prague by two secret Czech agents, as I stated earlier. But of course, the danger was by no means over, and Stienek still insisted that Ewald and I stay with him during a raid by Gestapo commandos.

My cousin Ewald suffered from painful ear infections—a pathetic, sad little *boychickl*. I continually ran a low-grade fever and had chills and arthritic pains in my limbs. The fleas gnawed at our ankles when they discovered that there were warm bodies above the barn, as well as below. No matter how much we cleaned and hung out our bedding when weather permitted, we could not evict those agile little pests. There were no bathroom facilities in the barn. We had to use chamber pots and then empty them in the outhouse behind the barn. Yuck!

Steinek provided us with a bathtub made out of wooden boards. You had to be mighty careful not to end up with a splinter in your tush (your backside). Water had to be fetched at the well with buckets, carried into the barn, and heated on the top of the small stove. Just like cavemen in prehistoric times, I thought. My parents and I were spoiled. Our city apartment was very modern, with running water, a state-of-the-art kitchen, and a hot water heater you lit before taking a bath.

It was always cold and drafty in the room above the barn because there was only that small stove in that large chamber. We heated hot water bottles before we went to bed. They warmed the space under our thick feather beds for a couple of hours. It felt heavenly!

The winter months were incredibly long and uneventful. I was nine years old and did not attend school, partly because I was not well and because I didn't speak the Czech language well enough, as we only spoke German in the parental home. Besides that, I had been called names by some of the children. "*Blba Nemzie*" (Stupid German) was one of them. To this day, I wonder why my parents didn't raise me bilingual; why they didn't make me tough! Better prepared.

One night, when my fever was dangerously high, I was transported in someone's car to the Fischer home in Prague, where a doctor administered a penicillin shot to treat the strep infection. I had a joyous reunion with my grandparents and Tante Erna. We stayed with them for several days. I received another antibiotic shot before returning to the village.

The Fischer family presented me with a white rabbit-fur coat, which had a matching muff, for the purpose of having my picture taken. I was so embarrassed! Pani, Mrs. Fischer, wanted me to call her Tante Emma, also treated me to a Shirley Temple movie in the German language. We walked the streets of Prague during the Nazi occupation to get to the movie theater. No one bothered us. Was it worth taking such a risky journey? I thought it was and was convinced that I looked like Shirley Temple.

These were the events of the first winter with our Czech relatives. In early spring, the unpaved roads were impossible for travel. So deep was the mud from the spring melt and the rainy period in April, that you lost your boots if the laces were not tight enough. But eventually, the mud turned into hard crevasses.

The Root Cellar

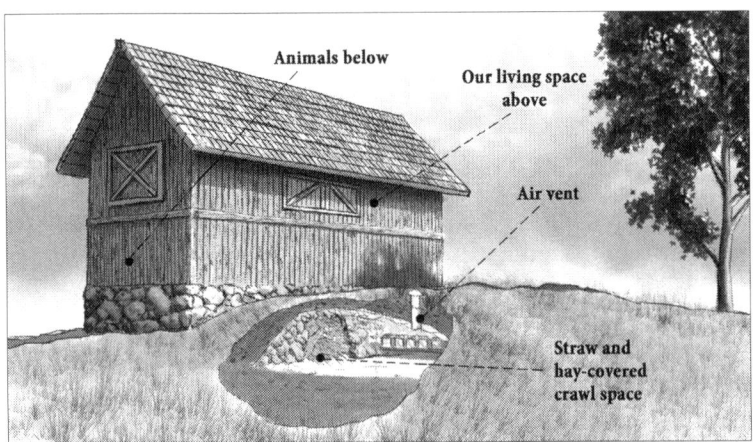

When German soldiers were near, we hid in the disused root cellar beside the barn. The air vent was masked by tall grass. Sitting in the darkness, we heard the soldiers and their dogs calling and barking as they moved about the farmyard above us.

Chapter 11
SS Soldiers Are Approaching!

ONE SUNNY MORNING IN MARCH, a few boys were running and shouting up and down the road. "*Nemtzies, Nemtzies!* Germans, Germans!" Jaro, Stienek's oldest son, came running up the steps to tell us. Papa hadn't put on his prostheses yet, and we all ran around hysterically screaming orders at each other, even though we had practiced our routine countless times. "Quick, quick, hide any incriminating belongings!" These would have been most probably any papers and documents from our town house in Sudetenland, and our family pictures.

We finally ascended the stairs into the barn, where behind a pile of hay we crawled into a hole in the foundation of the barn that led to the fruit and root cellar. There had been a front door that led to the fruit cellar under the garden on the hill with an exhaust pipe for oxygen supply hidden among the vegetation. But Stienek had sealed the front entrance of the storage unit with a layer of cement and smeared dirt over it, then loosened the rocks in the foundation of the barn and made a narrow crawl space to access the fruit cellar. He always piled straw or hay to hide the opening after we entered. We hadn't given it a thought that there was no back entrance—we were just grateful to be safe. Jaro, Stienek's fourteen-year-old son, tall for his age, slipped in right behind us.

After the Nazi occupation of Bohemia, the German soldiers had begun to round up young Czech males between the ages of fourteen and fifty for forced labor to work in appalling conditions in German factories, and Jaro didn't want to be among them. Stienek was right behind us, piling hay and straw high enough to conceal the opening. True, because our last name, Peska, was the same as our cousin Stienek's, we no doubt blended in with the village population, but Papa was rightly afraid that his condition of invalidism might be a dead giveaway.

The shelter was dark and damp. "Did anyone bring a flashlight?" It smelled of worms and rotting potatoes. We sat on crates and shivered with fear. My knees were shaking, my heart was pounding, and I held my breath until I was red in the face, and I was consumed by fright of an unknown enemy. "*Shhh, sei still,*" we told each other.

We huddled together for I don't know how long, waiting for someone to give us the signal to emerge out of that hole that could have easily become our coffin. As we were sitting in that dark cavity under the earth, I compared myself with a rabbit in a burrow. They run fast when they are being chased and disappear quickly into their underground holes. "Just like us," I told myself. "We are safe." Needless to say, I was even at age nine, very immature.

After we emerged, we were told that the SS or Gestapo troopers stopped at a few houses and hung around for a while conversing with a couple of *slecnas* (young women). Perhaps they were just hungry? On the other hand, could they have been searching for us? They were also known to relieve farmers of eggs, butter, cheese, and flour. The peasants didn't dare refuse.

The animals were now grazing in the fields, and the chickens, ducks, and geese noisily congregated in the courtyards of the farms. Pink, purple, and white heather bloomed in the outlying fields. You couldn't miss the aromatic, hardy chamomile flowers that grew profusely at the edge of the roads. That smell always reminded me of toothaches or stomach aches.

You were served chamomile tea for stomach ailments, and for a toothache, you boiled the blossoms, put them in a little muslin sack, and while they were still hot, you held it against your cheek. Did that potion work? Not to my knowledge!

I once listened to a lively song on the short wave radio. Marika Rökk was singing. Who was she? German and very famous. I always thought her name was sort of catchy. And the melody and the lyrics of the song are vivid in my memory: "*Im leben geht Alles vorüber, es geht Alles vorbei, nach jedem December kommt wieder ein Mai.*" (Everything passes by, everything will go away, after each December there will again come a month of May.) Perhaps the song lyrics were meant to be a feeble reassurance that the war would be over soon and the warm sunshine in the month of May would heal all wounds. The truth is that Hitler's malignant atrocities left gaping wounds that will never heal!

I also loved to listen to Mozart, Beethoven, and Haydn, and one of my all-time favorites was Jack Offenbach's composition of *The Poet and the Peasant*. Radio was mostly announcements from the propaganda ministries of the Third Reich boasting about military advancements in Russia, playing nationalistic marching songs, repeating Hitler's speeches, as well as classical selections of the great German masters. Papa, with his ears close to the short-wave radio they had brought along, was also able to tune in very discreetly to a partisan-resistance channel that gave us hope for an eventual end to all the madness.

During the summer of 1943, SS troopers again came to our hamlet a couple of times, poking around, looking for suspicious surroundings and any odd behavior. We were in the woods picking berries and mushrooms at this time. The Nazis were hunting human game all over Europe in a strict and official way. "Was Onkel Franz still watching over us?" I asked myself over and over. I often wondered in whose house my piano stood. Who, if anyone, was harvesting Mama's and Tate's fruit? Perhaps the red-winged blackbirds inherited that domain on the Cherry Hill after all.

Papa's experience at the Welfare Department came to be very useful. He composed many letters of requests to the Czech authorities for the villagers asking for medical aid or pension benefits. Every now and then, the local priest, a kindly man in his forties who had taken a liking to Papa, would drive him to Prague.

He invited my grandfather to come along a couple of times, but Tate wasn't too enthusiastic about the idea of driving into town with the clergyman. Tate usually hitched a ride with one of the farmers who took produce to the market place in the outskirts of Prague. While there, Tate kept in touch with members of the Bund, the Jewish workers association. They did an exemplary job of assisting the escapees of Hitler. Prague was still a junction for refugees, thanks to the leniency of the Czech authorities and their friendship, even during the Nazi occupation. Not only could the Jews live in seclusion, but the Czechs and the Jews supported and protected each other against the common enemy. From 1942, Rabbi Weissmandl, along with the Czech Secret Service and the Jewish Workers' Association of the "Bund," helped to relocate, protect, or hide Jews, thanks to the leniency of the Nazi-occupied government under Emil Hácha and its compassionate attitudes. Perhaps many Jews, such as the Von Trapp family, walked the Alpine path into Italy or Switzerland.

Under the city of Prague there existed for hundreds of years an immense network of underground passageways, tunnels, and caves that served as secret meeting precincts and asylums for escapees and refugees. Czechoslovakia was not a nation of saints, but it was a land of human beings who saved thousands of Jewish lives. Need I repeat once again, almost all the Czechs, at least the Bohemians, were united in the refusal to hand over the Jews to the Nazis? Of course, there might have been a few despicable exceptions in Slovakia, Hungary, and Carpathia.

One day, Papa returned from Prague with something "up his sleeve." He had secretly been in touch with the Communist Party and had been asked by Victor Stern, or one of his associates, to join him in an attempt to escape to Russia.

"*Russland*?" My Mutti was horrified. Papa had lost a lot of weight during our exile. He was not capable of withstanding the challenges of the unknown circumstances we would encounter, and besides that, the war was raging at the Russian front. Many Jews were simply rounded up and killed like cattle on the eastern battlefields. Others were treated like slaves and made to labor in the work camps until they simply died. She told him, "You have a sick child, Julius, and we are not exactly a robust pioneering family, are we? We are better off staying right here in the village." She said, "I'd rather be a live peasant than a dead Communist!" After listening to Mutti, Papa reluctantly agreed with her.

It was suggested to us, as the crops were ripening, that we join the workers in the fields picking hops, harvesting sugar beets and sunflowers. That would also be the safest environment. I liked that plan! That was new and exciting. Each hop plant, as it grew, wound itself around a wire at least twenty feet in height that was attached to another wire system at the top holding all the rows in the field together. When the hops formed soft, puffy grape-like clusters, they were ready to be picked. You had to grab the vine and pull with all your strength until it fell around you like a soft blanket. Everyone had a stool and a basket where the plucked hops were deposited.

Picking hops was a repetitive, somewhat monotonous process, but it had its rewards. Papa said it was almost spiritual, like meditation. Few people in the fields conversed with each other, and because we were trying to keep a low profile by being productive, we were not inclined to speak. All you would hear was the buzzing of the insects and the German military aircraft overhead every now and then. Repetitively picking away at the hops, you were in a world of your own. It was hypnotic and sedating, and obviously, there was a good reason for it. Dried hops made into a tea can induce sleep. So there you are! We were literally drugged, just like Dorothy in *The Wizard of Oz*, for seventy years! I don't think there were many local breweries in the villages. After drying, the hops were surely taken via trucks or wagons to the world-famous breweries in Pilsen and Budweiser, in the province of Bohemia.

Mutti was no longer obsessed with my eating habits and the dark circles under my eyes. Life had become simpler for all of us. As a worker, you were entitled to oatmeal or cream of wheat for breakfast. At noon, food was brought to the fields on a wagon. It usually consisted of a thick slice of rye bread spread with butter or chicken fat (shmalz), or perhaps it was lard? My favorite lunch was an English muffin of sorts, piled high with a sweet poppy seed spread, and for supper, potato dumplings with fried onions, boiled potatoes, and cottage cheese, or an egg and bread soufflé. Barley and mushroom, pea, potato, garlic, and caraway seed soups were served often and—come to think of it— were quite healthy. It was like the holiday Tisha B'Av with its dairy meals every day! It is not that we have to eat milk dishes during the nine days of mourning, but we are not allowed to eat meat during that period of sadness. Meat is the food of celebration on holidays and on the Shabbat.

Tisha B'Av is the saddest day in the Jewish calendar. Commemorated as a twenty-five-hour fast, the Ninth of Av is the anniversary of the destruction of the First Temple, built by King David, and the capture by the Romans of Betar, the last Jewish fortress to hold out in the Bar Kokhba rebellion. In 135 CE, Betar was plowed up or plowed under and turned into a non-Jewish city on the Ninth of Av.

In 1492, the Ninth of Av was the last day by which all Jews either had to be baptized or leave Spain. Over 300,000 chose to leave, but many under the watchful eye of the Inquisition were caught and burned at the stake.

World War I began on the Ninth of Av. It uprooted many Jewish communities and brought on the Russian Revolution that crushed Judaism there and led to the massacres of Jews throughout the Ukraine in 1918-21.

To supply me with the necessary protein in my diet, Mutti used to steal an egg from under the chickens as often as she could. Papa then poked a hole in it, shook it up and made me drink it raw! Yuck! It's a miracle that I didn't perish of salmonella.

The drinks the farmers supplied were water to which they added apple cider vinegar. I wonder if they knew that the vinegar had large amounts of potassium, which energizes you and kills the bad bacteria in your digestive system, and also enzymes that help you digest your food? Once in a while, they even made a Schweinebraten, a pork roast with potato knödel and purple cabbage, which was a special treat among the Czech population. Did we eat the pork? Perhaps we may have eaten only the potato dumplings and the cabbage.

Some of the children in the village had bicycles. I begged my mother and father to get me one, but of course it could not be. Our lifestyle here could not be considered a normal one. I didn't socialize with any of the girls in the village. I always greeted the children with a polite "Dobre jitro," good morning, or "Dobre den," good day, and they just looked at me with big eyes. I easily became embarrassed when I spoke in my limited Czech tongue. The children no doubt thought I was a little strange, a bit odd. Did I feel they would recognize my looks or my actions to be those of a Jew? It crossed my naive mind only fleetingly. After all, I had little Jewish awareness.

I didn't necessarily associate lighting candles on Shabbat with Judaism, and besides that, after our flight from Schönpriesen we seldom practiced that ritual. I felt neither Jewish, nor German, nor Czech. I only felt that I didn't belong.

The disintegration of the secure, idealistic world that I had known in Sudetenland had left a void, an emptiness. All I knew for certain was that the ruling party and the fierce SS troopers were the enemy of the entire local population.

Submission

The priest suggested to my father that it would be wise for us to attend church services now and then to dwarf any suspicion. He also suggested baptism for Ewald and me. To keep us safe, he said. Was he just being a Mensch or did he intend to convert these Jewish souls to Catholicism? Did he think we were little vampires that needed to go through some form of exorcism? Mommy was in favor of anything that would keep me unharmed and preserve our camouflage, though she usually sent me to church with Tante Minkl.

I don't remember whether I was baptized or not. Baptism in the Catholic Church is not a ritual bath. You are not submerged but have only a dab of holy water placed on your head. My parents had to lay a foundation for me to live the life of a Christian, if necessary by studying Catechism. I had to be prepared to answer questions about my background and not be ignorant about the Catholic religion.

My mother washed and rinsed my hair with chamomile tea made from the chamomile flowers that grew abundantly in the area, usually on the side of the road. Chamomile tea was not only a popular healing agent, but it was also a bleaching agent for the hair, and it was easier to obtain than peroxide. I now looked so *Arisch*, Aryan, with my blond highlights!

After a while, the Pater Noster, the sign of the cross, and the Ave Maria became a familiar routine. In the humble little chapel, I was fascinated by the man nailed to the cross. Because I was bombarded by political opinions and theories most of my life, after learning the story of Jesus I came to the conclusion that he was perhaps the first Socialist. He wanted the wealthy *Kohanim* to share their resources with the less fortunate, the poor inhabitants of Jerusalem and the rest of Israel.

In the fall, we all helped our cousins with the preparation of canning fruits, making marmalade, and so forth. Nothing was wasted. When we peeled apples, the peels were not discarded. They were hung over strings above the stove to dry, just like Mama used to do. It could even have been her idea. In the winter, we made tea from the apple skins, laced with nutmeg.

Incidentally, every time we left the room above the barn for any length of time, I was in charge of hiding our personal belongings, such as books and photos, under the floorboards, and then covering them with straw.

During the summer of 1943, the SS troopers came to our hamlet a couple of times, poking around, no doubt collecting much-needed edibles because food was beginning to get scarce for everyone. We were in the fields each time, *Boruch Hashem*! Thank God. At the end of the year 1943, Roosevelt announced via short-wave radio that the Germans would surely be defeated soon, and indeed they were less successful at the front lines east and west of our hideout.

For many years, I was not aware that my parents planned not to be among the unlucky ones to be taken to a concentration camp. Papa and Mutti had enough lethal pills to kill themselves painlessly. They were unwilling to relinquish control of their lives to the Nazis in a concentration camp. They secretly planned, in the worst scenario, to choose their own method of dying. I was to stay with Stienek and Elli, whom they had come to trust unconditionally. Would I have been raised as a Catholic? Perhaps not. Stienek was a "free thinker," a Humanist, and a Mensch.

It must have been a nightmarish state of mind for my parents to be in. But they were two extraordinary human beings, resilient and courageous, and I don't believe that they could have said "*Servus, Adieo*, so long, see you later," to their only daughter. I believe they would have chosen life, as opposed to committing that fatalistic act of self-destruction.

We managed to go to Prague once more despite the risks involved. Tante Erna introduced us to a dark-haired man who came from the province of Slovakia. His name was Pepic Rehak, supposedly Jewish. Mr. Rehak was a partisan for an underground movement fighting against the Nazis at the Polish border. He was tall and dark and

Leah, wearing a rabbit-fur coat, attended a Shirley Temple movie with the Fisher family in Prague, under the noses of Gestapo officers, in 1942.

looked like a Romani to me. The horror stories he narrated about the mass killings of civilians he had witnessed in the mountain villages made my hair stand on end and gave me nightmares again. He called me "Yanah." My legal name, Liane, translated into Czech, would have been Lyanah.

Papa was not feeling his usual cheery self on the way back. The mental and physical tensions were beginning to take their toll. It was not just the north wind that sent shudders through his frail body, but also the horror stories that constantly reached his ears. He was somewhat relieved to have heard about the Germans surrendering to the Russians in the city of Stalingrad, which they had conquered and occupied. The Germans were starving and freezing and out of ammunition, a feat the Russians accomplished by completely surrounding the city. Hurray!

In contrast, there was distressing news about the *Warschau* (Warsaw) ghetto and our people fighting the Nazis to the end. They say this is because they knew that if they didn't die in their homes or in the sewers beneath the city, they would surely die in the concentration camps. Papa heard they had few guns, but what they lacked in firepower, they made up in ingenuity. He said, "If I had a healthy body, I would join the Partizans that desperately fight against the Nazis." It sure sounded like Papa was no longer a pacifist.

Rumors spread about the killings in the concentration camps. Papa said: "What kind of nightmare is being acted out before our eyes? Why is Judaism again being dragged before the courts of the Fascists? Haven't the Germans noticed how adaptable we had become in the last hundred years? Did we not show our gratitude and admiration for their historical ideals, their culture, by embracing the German writers, poets, and composers, such as Mozart, Beethoven, and Goethe?"

Why does the whole world stand by silently and passively and let these indescribable horrors take place? Were the rumors they heard not taken seriously? One can forgive the uninformed for their ignorance and perhaps the individuals of the countries that Hitler occupied that were paralyzed by fear, but what about their leaders? What of the American government and the heads of our American Jewish organizations? Jewish Zionist organizations from Britain and

South Africa responded, sent representatives, and started *kinder* transports. Except for Agudath Yisroel, American Jews did not.

On a sunny day in January of 1944, the German soldiers this time came with heavy trucks, machine guns, and dogs. I assume that they were getting desperate. They went from house to house shouting accusations at residents, demanding food and alcoholic beverages. The guttural, harsh sounds of the *Hochdeutschen* language penetrated the walls of our underground shelter. Were they looking for us? Would they finally find us this time? We could hear men shouting and dogs barking, not sure whether they were theirs or ours. Our *Mama loshen*, mother tongue, although German also, had a softer pronunciation, more like Hebrew, Yiddish, or French. A raw German accent still makes me shudder!

The assailants seemingly stayed for hours, and each hour was more unnerving than the one before. We were afraid to move about or carry on a conversation. We only whispered and prayed. "*Sei still*" was the advice given. You didn't get used to the spiders or the mice and rats scurrying across your body. I still become hysterical when I see a spider! You didn't dare light a candle. We feared that the fumes, the smell of the wax, might be detected by the dogs on the other side of the crawl space.

It was always alarming when the SS soldiers hung around too long and entirely possible that, had they known we were under the protection of the priest and the villagers, they could have and would have herded everyone into the chapel and burned it down with everybody in it. The Nazis had been known to do just that in France and in Russia. "*Schweig, sei still*" always came to mind and holding my breath became a habit. Perhaps I assumed that it may bring a halt to these insane experiences.

My Mama's and Tate's Wisdom

My family members tried their best to normalize our everyday existence, so storytelling was to become one of our favorite pastimes. My grandmother remembered an incident of a childhood experience during her stay in an orphanage when someone stole a piece of bread she had hidden under her pillow. She said she cried bitterly, perhaps not just over the morsel of food, but at six years old, she must have been frightened and missing her family members. Poor little girl! Mama pointed out to me how very fortunate we were in many respects. God was watching over us, and we had the unconditional support of family and friends.

One other story stands out in my memory. When Mama and Tate were young, they attended an illusionist's performance at the city theater. This entertainer, a mass hypnotist, convinced about ninety percent of the audience that because of a cloud burst, water was rushing into the auditorium, rising higher and higher. People were screaming hysterically, jumping on top of seats in fear of drowning. As soon as the performer lifted his spell, everyone found the experience amusing and entertaining.

But, Mama said, the incident was frightening, to see how the power of suggestion of one man can influence so many individuals. She pointed out that governments and their leaders were capable of achieving that process as well. They can indoctrinate and brainwash the receptive, unsophisticated minds of the masses, just as Hitler had convinced his people that the Jews were subhuman creatures and were the enemy of the German nation.

Tate spoke about many amazing and sometimes bizarre experiences that occurred during his duty in the military service under Kaiser Franz Joseph on the Serbian and Russian front. He told us about the Mameluks—I believe the Mameluks were the Turks from the Ottoman Empire—and how skilled they were in the art of knife throwing. I would then go outside and try to perfect my aim at the wooden fence with Papa's pocketknife. I begged my Tate to tell me the stories of the book *Arabian Nights* and of "Ali Baba and the Forty Thieves" over and over. And he always did.

One of Tate's experiences that I found particularly astonishing happened on the Russian front. During the daily ceasefire period, the *Mittagstunde*, the noon hour or perhaps at sundown, the solders from both sides, the Austro-Hungarians and the Russians, very honorably followed that ritual truce. During that pause, the men from both sides often sat on the branches of the same trees in the same orchard to enjoy the supplements of the fruit, and they actually conversed with each other, laughing and telling jokes. How was that for camaraderie among enemies? Just one more example of who makes the decisions to declare war.

My Tante Erna told us stories of effective and satisfying ways of "playing dumb" with the Gestapo in Prague. When they raided apartments in multiracial neighborhoods and inquired about the whereabouts of specific Jewish families, the Czechs would say: "Oh, they left. We have no idea where they went. They were Jewish? We didn't know that!" The Czech population was known for their diplomacy and cleverness.

By this time, I was ten years old. During all those months in exile, Papa and I continued our homeschooling, though we lacked the essential learning tools. My grandmother tried to teach me how to knit and crochet. It was a satisfying hobby. I guess Mama encouraged those seemingly useless "keep busy" activities such as needlework because she wanted to prevent me from going stir crazy during those long winter months. Mama and my Mutti didn't have a sewing machine anymore, so they sewed by hand, quickly and skillfully, and in the process taught me that practical skill as well.

Since Onkel Joseph, Tante Minkl's husband, came to join us, the atmosphere in our cramped quarters was not always harmonious. Onkel Joseph was a mathematics teacher and very regimented and persnickety about everything. I'm not sure where he hid before he joined us. In my opinion, he might have been a deserter of the German Army. No one ever spoke about it. His space was always tidy and well organized, which I admired. He was obsessed with the cluster flies and with cleaning everyone's shoes daily, as if it really mattered on these unpaved roads. On the other hand, it gave him something worthwhile to piddle with. Papa and he disagreed on child-rearing issues and their psychological consequences.

Onkel Joseph was a Sigmund Freud *Anhanger*, disciple, and Papa agreed more with Alfred Adler, also an Austrian Jew and psychiatrist. In Adler's analysis, he found that, in an individual's development, an inferiority complex was the basis of becoming a dysfunctional human being. I quite agree with that thought.

One day, in the spring of 1944, when Tante Minkl, my cousin Ewald, and I went for a walk in the fields, Minkl said: "Shhh! Listen! *Sei still!*"

I heard the wind in the trees, the wheels of a wagon squeaking, a jack-rabbit quietly hopping through the tall grass, the faint gurgling of a nearby brook, and the barking of a dog in the village. And then we heard it! A distant rumbling coming from the northeastern sky. What was that foreboding sound? Could it be an approaching thunderstorm? A chill went through me, and my knees were shaking, I held my breath again, and Tante Minkl went pale. "Please don't faint, Tante Minkl!" From that day on we heard hollow roaring sounds in the still of the night, never knowing whether it was friend or foe on our heels.

In the days to come, the sounds became more distinctive, and one was certain that it came from bombs and cannons. To this day, I become frightened when I hear the rumbling of an approaching thunderstorm. During those moments of flashback, I again feel all alone, no one to share my thoughts with. It sends shivers throughout my soul, and I fear, based on the latest news reports, that humanity seems doomed, because it does more evil than good.

Chapter 12
Spiritual Thoughts

BECAUSE I WAS DEPRIVED OF A RELIGIOUS ELEMENT in my daily life, I craved the spiritual discipline. That environment would have enriched my days. Just imagine what a treasure of knowledge, understanding, faith, security, intellect, and essence we could have obtained from that manual, the *Chumash*!

Up to now, I've concentrated on the Assimilation, Realism, and the Zionist movement that the Bohemian Jews were more familiar with and which were very influential in my development. I'm sure that we've all concluded that the religious element is definitely the distinguishing mark of the Jew, and with the help of Felix Weltsch and my other Bohemian friends, we will look into the diversity of the Jewish religious practices.

Within the Austro-Hungarian Empire there developed a Bohemian, Moravian, and Silesian Jewry that I grew up with and a Hungarian Jewry to which the Slovakian and Subcarpathian Ruthenia belonged. Their orientation and practices definitely set them apart. The Jews in the western regions were secularized in their outlook on life, whereas the Subcarpathian Ruthenia provinces were populated by the Orthodox and Hassidic Jews.

In the 19th century, the Hungarian administration shamelessly neglected the mainstream regions of Subcarpathian Ruthenia. Not much was done for the economic, the educational, or the cultural needs or development for the Jews in that region. Hunger, deprivation, and dire poverty reigned in the rural areas, where two-thirds of the isolated Jewish communities made their home for perhaps hundreds of years.

Messianic yearnings were aroused to mystical exultations by the influence of the Frankist movement and further awakened by the Baal Shem Tov, the founder of Hassidism. When the door was opened to the secular West, after the establishment of Czechoslovakia, the Subcarpathian Ruthenia self-contained Hassidic world found it difficult to interact with the declining religious and political issues in the Bohemian and Moravian districts.

The rabbis in their wisdom strove to guide their flocks both in cities and villages into congregations and in this manner they established a serious and conscientious society. They built *mikvas*, ritual baths, and synagogues and brought the young people together with songs and prayers to observe Shabbat and the Holy Days. The famous community of Mukcevo was home to many famous rabbis. Rabbi Joseph Meir Weiss, a great Hebrew scholar and author of significant books, had considerable influence on the people in the small villages. Rav Joel Teitelbaum, who resided in Szatmar at the Rumanian border and later lived in Williamsburg, Brooklyn, surely left his mark forever in history as the "Szatmar Rebbe."

The rabbis of that region took over the children's education as well as the needs of the adults. Their followers accepted their demand for modest clothing and strict *kashrut*.

Among the Hassidim, the gestures of daily life were not empty ones. Each prayer, every move and act, was to demonstrate the splendor of Hashem from the opening of one's eyes in the morning to the moment of falling asleep at night. That *Weltanschaung*, philosophy of life, definitely would have appealed to me as a child.

The strongest instrument that gradually remolded the Jewish communities into permanent parts of Jewry was the rabbinical scholar. In the old ghettos the rabbi was the sun, and the yeshiva was the radiant light that surrounded him, and it was not the number of students or the wealth of its members, but the spiritual greatness of the rabbi that brought honor to his yeshiva.

The Slovak Yeshiva of Bratislava-Pressburg had the largest number of students and the greatest fame, spreading beyond its borders to Austria, Germany, Hungary, Rumania, Yugoslavia, and even Switzerland and England. Rabbi Moses Schreiber, the *Hatam Sofer,* made it the Pressburg Yeshiva, and it continues under that name in Jerusalem.

One of the last leaders who headed the Congress Congregation of Pressburg from 1923 until the outbreak of World War II was Victor Stein. He combined a modern approach with an admirable blend of qualities that befitted the *Parnas* and *Rosh Knesset.* Many a philanthropic and cultural institution owed their establishment to him.

Without my Papa's analytical mind, I am not certain what Victor Stein's philosophy was, but I will give it my best effort.

Under the leadership of President Masaryk, Czechoslovakia was influenced by American concepts. It laid the groundwork of democratic freedom and a pluralistic society. It spurred interest for Jews to enter into politics, agriculture, manual labor, and aroused strong nationalism among our young people, without whom we could not have conquered our land of Israel.

When Victor Stein accepted the presidency of the Congress Congregation, he summed up his philosophy of Jewish public life. Thanks to the diligent research of Hugo Stransky, we know what this great leader's opinions were. "We, the members of this Congregation, are progressive Jews, but not Jewish progressives. We want to continue toward progress in Judaism and not away from it."

He believed that a degree of flexibility was necessary towards advancement, towards moving forward with intellectual thought. He also believed that the rigid complexities of only clinging to the past were not improving the chances of the survival of World Jewry.

These progressive thoughts were bitterly denounced and resisted by many Orthodox congregations, all of whom were threatened by rational progressiveness.

I know that my parents were impressed by Victor Stein's logic and had it not been for the interruption of the Second World War, perhaps Papa and Mutti might have developed into becoming more observant Jews. They surely did not lack the moral, ethical, or spiritual qualifications, but regrettably, our Jewish connection was broken by the war and the consequences of it that determined our future.

Another *edler Mensch* worth remembering is Rabbi Weissmandl. During those final years before the Holocaust, in 1941 and 1942, he helped organize an underground railroad where Polish Jews were brought to Slovakia and from there to Hungary, which was still considered relatively safe at that time. The committee led by Weissmandl actually managed to stop the deportation of Jews to work camps for a time in 1942, during which time a considerable number of Jews were successful in escaping or finding shelter, just as our family was able to do, in order to survive the Holocaust.

Zionism

Zionism was a topic that my Papa examined thoroughly as well. Its roots go back to the sixth century BCE, when Jeremiah and other prophets implanted the idea of the hope of returning to Palestine among their people living in exile. Often through the centuries, self-proclaimed Messiahs had tried to organize mass movements that failed. So Zionism did not come to fruition until a contemporary movement began under the influence of Haskala, enlightenment.

The movement was started by the German-Jewish philosopher Moses Mendelsohn in the eighteenth century. Jews tended to become more worldly and less religious. They were inclined to look at action rather than prayer for the solution of their problems. Theodor Herzl organized such a movement at the end of the nineteenth century. In 1907, Bohemian Zionists established their own weekly newspaper in the German language, called *Die Sebstwehr*, self-defense. It became the foremost periodical in Czechoslovakia, and its representative from our district of Aussig was Hugo Stern.

Chaim Weizmann, who became the first president of Israel, had joined the Zionist movement as early as 1904. He served as a delegate to numerous congresses of the world's Zionist organizations. In 1917, the British government issued the celebrated Balfour Declaration, which eventually led toward the establishment of a national home for the Jewish people.

Also worth speaking of is the Women's Zionist Organization, which had its beginnings in Prague, Bohemia in the year of 1900. Included in its program was the revival of the observance of Jewish holidays, organization of classes in the Hebrew language and raising money for the Jewish National Fund. It was of no surprise that the first Jew from Bohemia to settle in Palestine was a member of the Jewish National Fund. By her *Aliyah* in 1913 Martha Schick created a stir in Prague society. Many followed her example in the years ahead.

Also tied to the growth of Zionism in Czechoslovakia was the Women's International Zionist Organization, WIZO, of which Marie Schmolker was a valuable addition. She came from an assimilated Czech-Jewish background. When in 1933 the Jewish refugees came streaming into Prague, they found Marie ready to give them aid and protection. In 1939, she was arrested by the Gestapo and thrown into Pankrats penitentiary only to be released a few months later. She and Hanna Steiner bravely and tirelessly worked on behalf of their people during the Nazi occupation and saved thousands of Jewish lives. In addition, WIZO sent cables to London, the United States, and the Union of South Africa, urging them that everything possible had to be done to protest the annihilation of the Jews of Czechoslovakia. Marie Schmolker was a remarkable lady.

The ultra-Orthodox Jews, while believing in the ultimate restoration of *Eretz Yisrael*, the land of Israel, found the atheistic element of the organizations of WIZO and JNF unacceptable, even for the sake of the Jewish future. The Orthodox view was that we were not justified in aiming at the restoration of a Jewish nation. Their view was to wait for the coming of the Messiah and to rely only on God to bring His people back in His own time and with His own hands.

Because of this controversy, it was up to the Zionist organizations to convince the religious movement by the establishment of *Mizrahi*. It was able to succeed in many fields, such as the acceptance of the observation of Shabbat and the adherence to kashruth in Zionist activities. Mizrahi became the religious Zionist group whose motto was "*Eretz Yisroel le-am Yisroel al pi Torat Yisroel*," "The land of Israel, for the people of Israel in accordance with the Torah of Israel." *Agudath Yisroel* is another worldwide organization that originally took an anti-Zionist position. However, it eventually aided the settlement of religious Jews in pre-Israel Palestine.

Today, the Orthodox are represented in the Knesset, the Parliament in the State of Israel. Most of the Agudath branches were in Slovakia, and their headquarters were in Bratislava. Their social groups provided spiritual, moral, and financial support; they sponsored vacation trips for undernourished refugee children and, in addition, housed and supplied food, fuel, and clothing for hundreds of refugees. Orthodox landowners gave temporary employment to observant young men who wanted to get training in agriculture before moving to Palestine. In 1937 Agudath Yisrael of Czechoslovakia received an honor. Hundreds of delegates representing almost thirty countries met in Marienbad, Bohemia, not too far from Schönpriesen.

Supplying reasons for praising the multifaceted Bohemian Jew is an endless assignment that I am only too happy to elaborate on.

Another important fraternal order in Czechoslovakia was the Independent Order of *B'nai B'rith*, Sons of the Covenant. That organization had lodges in Prague, Karlsbad, Reichenberg, Brunn, Budweis, and Teplitz-Schönau, where my great-grandmother Shoshannah lived. The B'nai B'rith's objectives were to strengthen the spiritual and moral principles of our co-religionists, to impress upon them the worthy principles of love of mankind, to support the arts and sciences, to bring relief to the poor, to visit and care for the sick and to offer assistance to victims of persecution. Very noble ideals, indeed!

The B'nai B'rith lodges in Czechoslovakia, unlike those in the United States, were very exclusive. Applicants for membership had to meet rigid social and cultural qualifications and had to be approved by secret ballot, which gives the impression that the group might have been more than a little snobbish.

My great-grandmother fantasized about becoming a member of this exclusive society. But even if Shoshannah had possessed the proper *Yiches*, family prestige, she might not have been able to spare the one hundred and fifty Kronen induction fee. Hort, a sister organization of B'nai B'rith, was always on my Babbi's lips as well, and she spoke of all the generous contributions that were given by them to the needy and the widows. Receiving aid from these lofty organizations was probably as close as she got to them, although she certainly was an honorable, principled lady.

The popular Friendship Club that my mother belonged to in South Bend, Indiana, was established in Teplitz-Schönau, Bohemia, in the year of 1912, and was similar in rituals and ethics to B'nai B'rith.

Just recently I reread Rabbi Berel Wein's book, *Triumph of Survival*. He states, with legitimate reason I suppose, that the non-Jewish Jews, the secular Jews who were members and in many cases were leaders of the Socialist Party, held blind hatred against their own traditions, their own people, and especially against those of the Orthodox movement.

I had never seen the Socialist cause in that light, had never looked at it from that perspective. I do think that "hatred" is too strong a word and certainly cannot be applied in each case. My father simply did not have that negative characteristic in his gene pool.

My Papa's motivation was to find a path out of the canyons of dire poverty that the proletarians, the working class, were imprisoned in for so many years under the Kaiser's imperialistic system. I do agree with Rabbi Wein's belief that Socialism, because it discourages religious affiliation, promotes assimilation, and the fruits of that concept were very bitter ones in the decades to come.

Although sports and gymnastics never played a major role in the lives of the Jewish people, physical survival, especially with the revival of Zionism, started up the sports activities. They developed and formed the Maccabee Association and regarded their activities as the best means to improve physical fitness. The Maccabees took part in all winter sports, as well as track, soccer, swimming, field and ice hockey, tennis, rowing, canoeing, fencing, and horse racing. The Maccabee Association in Czechoslovakia alone had eighty-two societies and over ten thousand members!

Even in the field of aviation can the Bohemians boast! An outstanding aeronautical scientist, Karl Arnstein, a resident of Prague, was chief designer and constructor of the *Luftschiffahrts-Gesellschaft* Zeppelin in Friedrichshafen, Germany. He built forty airships, among them the famous *Graf Zeppelin*. Seeing a *Luftschiff*, an airship, floating silently over our town of Schönpriesen, was one of the most amazing recollections of my childhood. The entire population assembled in the streets and watched in astonishment.

In 1924, Karl Arnstein went to Akron, Ohio, as Director of Research and Development of Airship Construction. He later was responsible for the construction of fighter planes for the US Navy as vice-president of the Goodyear Aircraft Corporation.

The Climax of World War II

In the year of 1944, Papa brought home a special gift just for me. It was an English grammar book. "In anticipation of Hitler losing the war," he stated. But Mutti laughed at him and accused him of fantasizing. The Americans will never come as far as Czechoslovakia, and we should learn the Russian language instead! Still, Papa had a vision, and we began our studies in the English language. I now know that our pronunciation was not always correct, but we were making progress in reading and grammar.

I was eleven years old at that time and remember specific news bulletins that were announced on the shortwave radio, for instance: SS General Stropp boasted about his troops killing over fifty thousand Jews in the camps and on the road. Fifty thousand!? No doubt more like five hundred thousand or more. Not all of them died from bullets. Many committed suicide. How unbelievably tragic! All of my family members cried bitterly, including my proud Tate. Mama cried many tears about the disappearance of our Babbi.

Goebbels proudly announced that Berlin was now *Judenfrei*, free of Jews. Little did he know that eight thousand Jews still lived in Berlin during the war. Some of them were married to German spouses, and some survived in cellars and attics.

In that same year of 1944, the winter months were incessant. We all suffered from dysentery, throat and ear infections, and fevers accompanied by rheumatic pains. Recurring nightmarish staph infections that showed themselves as boils or furuncles also occurred. This painful condition was recurrent over the years and affected all the members of our family. But toothaches were the worst! I remember my Mutti sitting by the open oven door to be near the heat, with a small bag of hot boiled chamomile blossoms pressed against her swollen cheek.

That year was probably one of the most alarming. The Nazis in desperation began a new reign of terror in Hungary. They were rounding up Jews that had been relatively safe until now and transporting them to the Auschwitz gas chambers. In charge was Adolf Eichmann, better known as "the butcher."

Air traffic was on the increase, and the sky was dotted with flying objects. The German aircraft ordinarily flew low. I could, by the
sound of the motors, differentiate the Russian, German, and American fighter planes.

The Americans dropped loads of aluminum strips when they flew
overhead. The reason was that the enemy on the ground was blinded
by the metal ribbons glistening in the sun and therefore could not
easily spot the high-flying aircraft. Pretty clever! Leave it to the Americans! I excitedly ran around with my little cousin Ewald, picking
hands full of the shiny objects.

The Americans also dropped leaflets, giving us false hope of being liberated soon. Reports came over the *Welle*, the short wave radio,
that the German army had withdrawn their troops from France and
Belgium, as well as Poland. Were we to be next in line to be liberated?
We were dancing around in our room above the barn, making a bushel of *ayin horahs*, evil eyes.

The *Heide*, the moorland, was in bloom again, and the farmers were plowing their fields with the aid of their workhorses. The
earth smelled delicious. Whenever I could escape for a while, I loved
spending time in the wooded areas searching for the first spring flowers that sometimes hid under the dry leaves, or in climbing the black
walnut trees as high as I could, hoping to see beyond the horizon into
a different world.

Endless fields of poppies, white, purple, pink, and red, began to
blossom. The hops were chasing each other upward on the wire sys-
tems, and fields of sunflowers promised an abundant harvest.

I often wondered why they planted so many poppies across
Czechoslovakia. I know our cuisine included numerous dishes
made with those tiny little seeds. In Tante Erna's bakery, she made
donuts filled with a sweet poppy puree, *kuchens,* called *kulick-
ies*, which were small, round teacakes with poppy seed puree and
streusel on top. Then there were poppy seed strudels and even some
main dishes that my grandmother used to make, such as an oblong
potato *knedel*, called *Stupperlen*. I presume the expression comes
from cramming food down your throat. My Mama also called them
Schlishkes. The dumplings were then fried in butter and rolled in

crushed poppy seeds and sugar and sometimes in browned bread crumbs. Yum!

But how many poppy seeds can you eat? Mutti told me that the peasants boiled the hull or the shell, which contains opium, then sweetened it with sugar, and gave the liquid to their infants to relieve the symptoms of colic and in addition the mixture induced sleep. Well, that's one explanation! No wonder the Bohemians were so tolerant and happy-go-lucky.

On the radio, we heard about the shocking news about the concentration camp in Neidanek, Poland. After the Germans retreated, American and Russian reporters inspected the camp. One and one-half million people were put to death there. Staggering! Victims were Jewish men, women, and children, Romani, Jehovah's Witnesses, and other "undesirables" from every nation in Europe. With German efficiency, the prisoners were first stripped of their clothing and then herded into the next room, which was sealed, with the exception of holes placed in the ceiling.

From these openings, canisters of gas were tossed below. The warm showers that the victims took, first had opened their pores, allowing the gas to take effect more quickly. Prison guards watched through glass panes until all the people were dead. The bodies then were transported to a furnace. Teeth with gold fillings were knocked out and later sold. The crematorium could burn close to two thousand bodies a day. The ashes were sold as fertilizer to the German farmers. Every new discovery was worse than we already knew. There appeared to be no end to the horrors.

I am aware that not only we, the few survivors, but the whole world population has heard and read about these atrocities countless times. But were we not to repeat verbally and visually these documentations of barbarism, again and again, our grandchildren and great-grandchildren may get desensitized over time and, God forbid, forget. And we must never, ever forget!

We hadn't seen a German soldier for quite some time now. I'm sure they knew by then that all was lost, but it was also conceivable that the "werewolves," also known as the Hitler Jugend, were watching us from the forest behind the village. That very thought terrified me, and I held my breath, vowing to never venture into those woods again. All of us had erratic sleep patterns. I repeatedly had nightmares of hearses, funerals, and werewolves.

The Americans had achieved air superiority over the Nazis by the end of 1944. They bombed Berlin and Leipzig, but when they bombed Dresden, Papa said: "Dresden is not an industrial or a military town, all there are left are women and children. So why did they bomb the city so unmercifully with phosphor bombs for three days?" We heard the hollow roar in the distance and saw the red glow of the burning city in the northern sky for days.

We were very concerned about Tante Minkl, who was a very frail little lady, about 4'8" in stature. Her fainting spells became more and more frequent. "Minkl is definitely undernourished, and we have to make her well again," Mutti said. She then went from house to house, begging the farmers for eggs and butter. What we didn't know at the time was that Tante Minkl was carrying a child.

There was news on the radio that Churchill and Stalin agreed to divide Germany into two zones. Hello! The war is not over yet! Hitler had two more aces to be played. The V-1, a flying bomb carrying a ton of explosives, was aimed at England and killed almost three thousand people in one blow! The V-2s were faster and deadlier. Just think what he could have done with a stockpile of V-1s and V-2s. It was Hitler's last desperate move. Stienek said: "If they don't stop the Nazis soon, they may win the war yet!"

Thank God, the Americans finally landed in France. So many American soldiers laid down their lives for us at the great and infamous "Battle of Bulge." Hitler must have been delusional when he demanded that every man, woman, and child be armed as a last attempt at *Sieg*, victory, to fight to the end! Did his pathetic, crazed plan of the *Volksturm* ever come to fruition? Apparently not. Smelling Germany's demise, Hitler, the coward, committed suicide, in April of 1945. A few days later, the German Army surrendered unconditionally. The reign of the Swastika was over, and Hitler's dream of a 1,000-year empire.

Before Hitler committed that lily-livered act, he delivered a radio address to the German people, in which he accused them of disloyalty, and I clearly remember the words that he shouted, "*Ich werde meinen*

Volk keine traene nachweinen!" "I will not waste one tear on my dis-loyal nation!" He also vowed that within sixty years they would erect a monument in his honor. That date has long passed.

The nightmare had finally ended. We survived the Holocaust fore-most with God's help and good friends! Thank you, Hashem, Onkel Franz, Stienek, and Pater Hladikova, the priest in the village!

Chapter 13
Refugees Returning Home

We survived World War II. Papa, Leah, Mutti,
and in front, Mama, and Tate.

IN THE YEARS OF 1945—46, Soviet troops sweeping through Poland found thousands of victims on the road starving and dazed. Scenes of horror greeted the American troops when they opened the gates of Buchenwald. Slave laborers lying on their barrack bunks could barely lift their heads, their muscles eaten away. Maggots were visible in the corners of their sunken eyes as they watched silently the GIs that liberated them. Those victims were the lucky ones. They were the survivors.

Tante Minkl had just given birth to Mia, a quiet little girl, premature and barely alive. She didn't even cry at birth. Maybe she was afraid to be heard? Perhaps she heard the warning of "*sei still*" too many times? The experience of the birth was quite memorable and more than a little frightening for me. We waited for mother and daughter to be strong enough to travel.

Tante Erna and Pepic came to the village with a car to help drive us all to the train station in Prague. There were hundreds of people pushing and shoving, cheering and crying, heading north to an uncertain future. The train we boarded had a makeshift Communist star on the locomotive. Papa said he should have felt like Raskolnikov from Russia riding triumphantly in the front of the train, but there were no feelings of exultation, no victory celebrations, even though it was now again in vogue to be a Socialist.

At every junction, dozens of haggard, tired-looking individuals were trying to board the overloaded train. People were hanging from it like bunches of grapes. The countryside was uninteresting until we approached the Middle Mountains and the Elbe valley. "We are home again! *Mam Domu!*" We recognized a few familiar faces at the train terminal in Krasne Bresno, including Onkel Franz. He was crying when he saw my Papa. Franz was now on the other side of the fence, no doubt waiting for Papa's advice and protection.

The Czech population that was ousted by the Sudeten Nazi sympathizers now returned from the interior of Czechoslovakia and were more than ready to reclaim their possessions. Onkel Franz had cleared out our apartment and willingly returned our belongings. His wife and her father, the *Burgermeister*, the mayor, fled the area. Was Franz's father-in-law one of the individuals guilty of war crimes? Maybe not. Not every Nazi was. Was Onkel Franz involved? Was he a member of the Nazi party? We will never know. Perhaps Franz was an opportunist, but in my eyes he was a victim as well, who risked his own life to help his family members stay alive.

Mama and Tate's estate on the mountain was uninhabitable. The Nazis had exalted plans of erecting a training center for the Hitler *Jugend,* Youth, on top of that summit. They began to tear down part of the building, but their intention never came to fruition. No one maintained the property, and it took my grandparents many weeks to make it environmentally safe.

Food was scarce. The shelves in the stores were empty, except for items like vinegar, salt, and mustard. I once ate with a spoon a whole jar of mustard because it tasted so good and, needless to say, I was nauseous for a couple of days. My grandfather dug a bushel of potatoes and sugar beets out of some farmer's field. We cut up the sugar beets and boiled them for hours, if not days, and the end result was a jar of molasses that we served over the boiled potatoes. Not too tasty, I assure you. To this day, I cannot tolerate the taste of molasses, not even in cookies. Mutti said it was a nutritious meal that contained calcium, potassium, and iron. We ate a lot of watery soups made of rutabagas and potatoes that we dug out of the ground, and the fruit on my grandparents' trees kept us alive.

We gathered the remnants of the grain harvest in the fields, but that task proved to be backbreaking labor. Our Tate had a better idea, by going on the unharvested plots armed with a pair of shears, cutting the pods of the stalks of wheat, barley, rye, or oats. I recall helping to glean the grain from the husks. Mama ground them in the coffee grinder and made mush or bread from the whole wheat kernels.

Our friends assured us that the situation would improve when the Russian army arrived. We will all be entitled to UNRA, United Nations Relief rations, and then we'll be able to make bread again, they naively declared.

Why didn't we go to the Jewish Welfare system? Were they even operating in the anarchistic conflict at that time? I am sure that it was. Was the reason foolishness, ignorance, or pride on our part? This reminds me of my mother's famous quotation, "Foolishness and pride grow on one tree." That pearl of wisdom might have originated during those troubled times.

Yes, the postwar years were by no means easy or unchallenging, but our day-to-day existence was no longer life-threatening, and one had to be grateful for that. On the other hand, it felt like the world was collapsing around us and on top of us. What challenges will torment us now? We, the Jews, particularly the secular ones, who like me, lost their inner core of Jewishness? To the point of self-hatred?

My dream came true! I got to ride Tante Erna's bicycle. It only took a few days for me to learn how to balance on it and I felt like I was born again, riding through every street in town, up the steep hill of the Kellerstrasse where the Steiner family used to live. I wondered if they had survived the war in Hungary.

I raced with the bike around the cemetery, where I stopped and visited Votta's grave, and down into the valley where I ran into a wall and chipped my front tooth. Mutti was very upset. I had to stop at Toni Siegel's farmyard to tease a turkey with a stick. Apparently, someone else lived there, and it wasn't Tony and Reze. They told me in no uncertain terms to never come back again. I'm not sure how the Siegels endured the war and wish I had asked Mutti and Papa, who took so many unanswered questions to their grave.

One evening, after a tremendous explosion, the sky was ablaze with fire, metal shrapnel flying all around us, and we concluded that the world was coming to an end after all. Someone had sabotaged the Nazi ammunition warehouse just outside of the city. Bombs, hand grenades, and dynamite ignited and injured dozens of people. Thank God, the storehouse was not in a populated area or in the hands of an enemy! The explosion left a huge crater.

Russian Invasion

Shortly after that fiasco, the Russian army arrived. An elite group came riding into the city on horseback, looking mighty dignified and exotic in their high collared, medal-laden uniforms. I ran with my cousin Ewald up to one of the officers and handed him a bouquet of wildflowers. He patted me on the head and lifted Ewald on top of his horse, only to release him again after he let him hold the reigns. By that time poor Tante Minkl was ready to faint again! I was mighty impressed with the Russians at age twelve. "They are our liberators, our friends," I decided.

The United Nations was established, with delegates of fifty nations, in the hope that it would be a new start to a way of lasting peace in the world. Another pipe dream!

In general, the Czech population was not happy over the Russian liberation. Already we had to hand over Ruthenia to the Communists.

After the elite group made their headquarters in Aussig, the infantry arrived with trucks and huge tanks and about one hundred horses. They were a completely alien assembly, looking much like a horde of Huns. They were of Mongolian descent. "No one won the war, only we Russians did!" they boasted, and for quite some time it surely looked that way.

The soldiers ransacked the local brewery and the fine liqueur reserves at the Zuckerfabrik. For days they pillaged the stores in drunken mobs and molested women regardless of age. If you had gold teeth, you were wise to keep your mouth closed. The drunken sieges seemed never-ending. It was not safe for women and children to be on the streets. Finally, their superiors were made aware of the outrageous behavior of their troops. Many soldiers were arrested, and the high-ranking officers apologized publicly for the terrible behavior of their soldiers.

Despite the fact that the local authorities tried to keep order, the Czech population revengefully looted the homes of many Germans. A couple of German war widows with their children had already committed suicide. But how can a parent make such a decision? To murder your own child? That news was very upsetting for me then, and now I find it even more unbelievable. In all fairness, I am trying to understand the SS widows committing that unspeakable, desperate act of taking the life of their children.

Was losing the war such an unacceptable tragedy? Did not only the death of their spouses but also the loss of their idol, their leader Adolf Hitler, contribute to their devastation? Enough reason to sacrifice their children? The war was over and, unlike the Jewish people, they did not have to fear the threat of concentration camps, slavery, or fiery furnaces. Their children could have grown up in a free world. I believe that those women were arrogant and spiritless.

A steady stream of refugees from Poland arrived in our town. We witnessed unbelievably heart-breaking scenes for many, many days. Some people dragged along on foot without shoes, rags wrapped around their feet. Some had pushcarts on which they transported their children or their aged parents. They rode on donkeys, on bicycles, on wheelbarrows; invalids were dragged along on makeshift stretchers. They brought along chickens in crates and goats to supply the necessary food for their children. Some hadn't eaten for days, and a hot bath was something they only dared to dream of. So much suffering because of one insane man!

The Czech authorities opened the schools, the theaters, and the train stations to house and feed that multitude, and as usual, they opened up their hearts and their pocketbooks as well. We also shared our flat with a few families. Some were Jewish and others were not. We had become cosmopolitan globe trotters, *Weltbürgers*! "Global citizens." Mutti and I helped at the public school with a group of other women, making soup, taking care of the sick, and playing games with the children. Chaos and bewilderment reigned.

Next on the agenda for the Czech people was the evacuation of the German Nationalists, the *Sudetendeutschen*, who had once been our friends. They were transported to the Russian-occupied zone of Germany and were only allowed to bring with them what they could carry. This did not include money or jewelry. In our opinion, that was more than justifiable. "Now they get their wish," Papa said. "*Heim ins Reich*! Home to the Empire!"

Bands of Romani roamed the neighborhoods, occupying vacant homes, sometimes moving their horses onto the ground floor and their families inhabiting the upstairs quarters. Some did their cooking over an open bonfire in someone's living room. If they were overcome by the smoke, the fumes, they cut a hole in the roof! I changed my childish mind about roaming with them after witnessing that fiasco. Anarchy reigned in the border regions of Czechoslovakia.

In my view, even in the 21st century, anarchy is a result of frustrated individuals' concerns not being acknowledged, and oppression, such as inequality of income, poverty, racial discrimination, criminal negligence, and a countless number of additional basic human rights issues, that are either overlooked or blatantly ignored.

Chapter 14
Leaving Our Cradle
of Bohemia

I WAS THIRTEEN YEARS OLD NOW and taller than Mutti. What I wouldn't have given to attend school, to have a group of friends to interact with! The streets were still unsafe and we seldom ventured out very far. They were lonely, lonely days. We played Chinese checkers for amusement and read to each other from old books.

Tante Erna was in the process of reopening her bakery with her new husband, Pepic Rehak. Mr. Rehak was a Zuckerbacker, a confectioner by profession, specializing in the creation of fancy French and Austrian tortes and pastries, unlike Tante Erna's first husband, Joseph Löebl, Uncle Seph, who was a bread connoisseur. Customers used to come from far and wide to buy his bread, his *Semmeln*, hard rolls, plain or with *Salz und Kummel*, salt and caraway seeds, as well as the Bohemian *Kulicki*, a small round yeast *Kuchen* with fruit, poppy seed paste, and streusel. Unfortunately, Uncle Seph died in 1941 on the Russian front, but the *Löebl Bäckerei* was in operation until 1942, when Tante Erna abandoned it to escape to Prague. But the saga of the bakery continued.

Rehak's bakery in Krasne Bresno never prospered under the Russian occupation. Despite the risks involved, Tante Erna and Pepic abandoned the property and fled the country across the Russian-German border in 1949, which was not as frequently patrolled then as was the

Erna, 1945, always smiling.

American-German section of the border. They somehow managed to cross the line to the American sector illegally, by train, through Berlin. They applied for a visa to Canada, where in 1955 they again tried their luck in establishing a *Konditerei*, a confectionary bakery and coffee house on King Street, in Hamilton, Ontario. Pepic's bakery was quite profitable and was still in operation in 1996, to my knowledge.

Tante Erna passed away in 1997, may she rest in peace. Sadly, she left no descendants. I miss her terribly. She visited the United States many times. Those visits were always eagerly looked forward to by my children and grandchildren. She had the talent of raising one's spirits with her unique sense of humor and sunny personality. We all remember her playing the guitar and singing one of her favorite songs, "Tom Dooley." And most important, and let's not forget, that she was a passionate supporter of Eretz Yisroel and the American way of life. She knew all the lyrics of our American Broadway musicals, but her favorite ballad was Neil Diamond's "Sweet Caroline." She will always be in our thoughts and in our hearts.

Einmal werde ich wegreisen
und nicht mehr wiederkommen
Einmal werde ich frei sein,
da zu gehen,
wo es keine Wege gibt.

*Tante Erna's death
announcement.*

*The card commemorating
Erna, who died suddenly
at the age of 76, reads:
One day I will go away
and no more return.
One day I will be free to go
where there are no roads.*

*A handwritten note with
the card says: "Tante Erna
was known for unpredictable,
rash decisions. She would
disappear and call you
three days later to tell you
that she is in Spain, or in
Yugoslavia, or in America
at Kennedy Airport. 'Could
you pick me up, Leah?'"*

The surviving Jews faced hard times again. No families waited for most of them. Their family members had either perished in the concentration camps or were scattered all over the world, they couldn't recover their properties, none of the Slavic countries welcomed them back, the Nazis confiscated their possessions during the war, and the Communists refused to return them after the war. But we lived. My survivor's guilt slipped back again. I have no idea why. Because I wasn't in a concentration camp? Because I didn't have a number tattooed on my arm? Even the workers in the German factories had a number tattooed on their arms.

Why did I feel guilty all these long years about staying alive?

In 1947, Papa was offered a position at the Welfare Department in Aussig, now Usti na Laben, in Czechoslovakia. He also contemplated being active again as a journalist or an editor but wasn't at all sure that he wanted to be that challenged in the unstable political atmosphere that existed at that time. He knew that the Czech government was increasingly controlled by Communist elements and he wanted no part of the dictatorship of Stalin's regime.

Papa, Mutti, and I, happy to be alive, in West Germany, 1949.

In one of his public addresses, Dr. Benes, the president, stated that he didn't trust the Soviet Union and was very concerned about his country's freedom. After Papa heard that announcement, he decided to leave Bohemia one way or another. "No more dictatorships," Papa said. Our ultimate goal and destination was to migrate to America.

Again, our Tante Erna saved the day! To obtain visas for immigration at the American Consulate in Prague, she stood in line for two days. She and hundreds of other refugees slept on the sidewalks and in doorways, so as not to lose their place in line. Finally, Tante Erna ran out of patience and let her sense of humor take over. She decided to faint and knew just how it's done professionally because she observed her sister Minkl's fainting spells all of her life. Her plan was successful. She was anxiously and caringly carried into the Consulate and given precedence to achieve her goals.

At the end of the year 1947, with a special visa but with heavy hearts, we left our beautiful town of Krasne Bresno. Our destination was the American zone, West Germany. And just in the nick of time! A few months later, in 1948, the doors to the West were closed when the Soviets commanded complete power over Czechoslovakia.

We were deposited in a holding camp at the border near the German Bohmerwald, where in a large warehouse building hundreds of wretched refugees laid around on American army cots, coming and going all day and all night. Dozens congregated around little stoves. So many crying children! Nauseating smells permeated the air. Mommy dabbed a little *Kölnisch Wasser* on my hair. We loved that aroma. Flowers and freshness! We were fed three meals a day. Barley with saccharine in the morning, watery barley soup at noon, and barley with nauseous pieces of pork fat for the evening meal, which we tried not to eat.

They warned us not to drink the water. Apparently, there had been a couple of cases of typhoid fever in the camp. Or was it cholera? Mutti was hysterical! Soap and hot water were limited in these cramped quarters, and head and body lice were thriving in that toxic environment. Body lice and bed bugs were the worst to get rid of. They lay their eggs in the seams of clothing, and after depositing their translucent eggs on your skin, the lice as well as the eggs extract your blood, grow round and plump, and leave red, sore spots all over your body. I shudder when I think about that experience.

Tante Minkl's little Mia, who was only about 18 months old at the time, came down with an ear infection in the holding camp. A compassionate woman gave Tante some warm oil to put into that *bubeleh's* (little doll's) throbbing ear. Much better now. At least a dozen languages were spoken in the camp, with refugees from Poland, Lithuania, Romania, Hungary, and Czechoslovakia coming and going all night long. We were speechless. I could tell by looking at Papa's face that all was not well. He was not sure that he had made the right decision.

Lager Lechfeld

At fourteen years old, awkward, painfully shy, a dropout in the art of social skills, I definitely deserved a failing mark in street smarts. After a harrowing three weeks of the indoctrination period, we were transported in a cattle car to Lager Lechfeld in Augsburg, Bavaria. I believe it was designated for mostly Jewish survivors and was under the supervision of the American government, where you were treated with respect, were given balanced meals, and were under a doctor's care.

Before we were assigned to our living quarters, we had to take showers. We, with many others, were led to a room and were told to shed our clothes. *Oy vey!* It couldn't possibly be—gas chambers? Well, no, of course not! It was, nevertheless, a devastating experience for me. You have to remember that in our society, modesty was a virtue you didn't have to be reminded of. I had never seen a nude person before and held my hands in front of my face, so as not to embarrass my mother and Tante Minkl.

Next came the medical clinic, where many American physicians and nurses examined dozens of individuals. Our English language skills were helpful, as few Americans spoke German or Czech. I complained of a backache, accompanied by a fever, and was diagnosed with a kidney infection. They also detected my heart murmur, a souvenir of the rheumatic fever. Mutti had a chronic cough, and after an X-ray was taken, they discovered spots on her lungs, which was a concern because she was exposed to tuberculosis by Tante Jenny when she was a child.

Papa was diagnosed with angina pectoris, high blood pressure, and irregular heartbeat. No medication was given. Poor Papa, his health broken by the starvation diet and the unspeakable stress he endured during two world wars. Could all that be at the root of the rheumatic arthritis that plagued all of us mercilessly and so cruelly for all these years?

We were taken to our barracks, where our accommodations were about twenty persons to a room. It appeared to me like a five-star hotel in comparison to the camp in the warehouse on the border! No privacy, but we knew the routine. We partitioned off our area with sheets and arranged our few belongings along the wall. Nutritious food was served in the "Mess Hall."

I wondered why it was called "Mess?" Didn't that word mean disorder? The offerings included lots of powdered eggs and various milk-related meals. I loved the macaroni and cheese, and the bean soup was tolerable but surely not as tasty as Mama's lentil or chicken soup. When we were served corn as a vegetable, we all looked at each other. *Mais?* Corn? We fed that to the chickens, didn't we? Apparently, my grandparents grew cow corn. *Leah! Beggars can't be choosers! How ungrateful I was!* Occasionally we were given Hershey bars. Yum! And gum. What is that?

We missed Mama and Tate terribly. They chose to stay in Russian-occupied Czechoslovakia with their youngest daughter, our Tante Erna. They wanted to be of assistance in her newly established bakery. But foremost, Mama didn't want to leave the area until she investigated our dear Babbi's disappearance. Surely, she thought, some administrative authority would come to her aid! It turned out to be a futile task to trace my great-grandmother's whereabouts. Her health in the year of 1941 was already fragile, and we know what Hitler did with the sick and the elderly.

At that time, few people realized that for every commonly known camp such as Auschwitz, Dachau, Theresienstadt, Bergen-Belsen, Buchenwald, and so on, there were hundreds of sub-camps, each placed meticulously into categories, such as care facilities for Germanization of foreign children who had desirable facial features and were later indoctrinated into German society; camps for pregnant mothers, whose offspring were used in experimental trials; camps for rebellious German and foreign youths; camps for the old and the weak, to be sooner or later disposed of. The list goes on and on, and ordinary citizens were not aware of these facilities that were spread all over Europe.

We hadn't heard from my Mama and Tate, and of course, that was very distressing. Letters written by us were returned at the Czech border. Are they safe? Are they well? Mutti and Tante Minkl worried themselves sick. I feared that Mutti would fall into one of her depressive states. Years before, she was diagnosed as suffering from depression. During that frame of mind, she always felt dejected and sad, and now she imagined the worst of circumstances surrounding her parents. I never learned how they escaped Czechoslovakia.

The Red Cross brought piles of second-hand *Schmattes*, old clothes. We were each allowed to select two complete outfits. The gray herringbone jumper stands out in my mind, and so does the blue wool sweater that itched unmercifully. I also picked a much-needed pair of winter boots. I had outgrown mine, so for a while, my Mutti and I shared a pair of boots, and when I occasionally accompanied Papa, she had to stay at the barracks.

Papa was continually writing letters, which was necessary, of course, and served the purpose of making him feel productive. He requested information from the Czech and the German government about a *Wiedergutmachungsrente* of some sort. The significance of that long word means "a pension to repay and or make good what we lost." Didn't we lose loved ones and all of our possessions because of that madman, Adolf Hitler? How can you put a price tag on a human life, on human suffering?

One day we heard Tante Minkl scream. After she saw Mia, my cousin, choking, she discovered a worm wiggling in her nose and managed to pull it out. It was ten centimeters long. The memory makes my flesh creep! Mia was taken by ambulance to a medical facility where they discovered that her digestive system was almost destroyed by the infestation of those atrocious, wretched worms.

The poor little girl was only two years old then, but throughout her life she was only able to digest baby food and the type of meals that astronauts are supplied with. Could Mia have ingested the worm larva at the holding camp on the border, where they served that nauseous barley mush with pork? Was Hitler the tyrant to blame for that gruesome plight as well? Of course!

We were in touch with Tante Fanny in America. Our hopes were high that we might emigrate to the United States and later to Israel.

But for now, in that spirit of adventure, the possibility of eventually migrating to the land of milk and honey made Papa and me daring and giddy. Our plan was to explore the city of Augsburg.

The city was founded by the Roman emperor Augustus, and from the twelfth to the sixteenth century, Augsburg had one of the most influential money markets of Europe. We hopped on a trolley car and got off at the market place. What an experience! Escapees, fortune hunters, and opportunists by the hundreds from India, Egypt, Italy, Russia, Hungary, Yugoslavia, and Turkey were all trying to make a living at the black market in this newly-found free market economy. If you had the funds, you were able to buy all the items you could not find in the stores, such as butter, sugar, coffee, toilet paper. "Toilet paper? What's that?"

Papa was excited. Characteristically tipping his hat, he approached a group of MPs, military police, that seemed oblivious to the presence of wheelers and dealers in their midst. He introduced himself and offered to paint or draw a portrait for a pitifully small amount of money. In fact, he sometimes painted a portrait for a pound of butter or a pound of coffee! After the first delivery, he was bombarded with dozens of contracts. Papa returned proudly to Lager Lechfeld with a new lease on life, another example of his determination and courage.

My mother, of course, was busy as well. She and a few Jewish and Christian friends industriously knitted sweaters and crocheted quilts for the American troops. The soldiers supplied the ladies with the necessary yarn, which was so soft and colorful. But I was not interested in knitting or crocheting. I wanted to attend school and interact with people my own age.

To be able to enroll in school, we had to be assigned to permanent living quarters first. During the post-war period, the German population was ordered by the government to share part of their living quarters, to house the thousands of refugees that were streaming into West Germany. So Papa and Uncle Joseph continued our home-schooling. Papa was my English teacher, and my uncle drilled me in my mathematics.

While in Lechfeld, we met many Landsmen, Czechoslovakians, among them the Steiner family. Their children, whom Tante Minkl had taken care of, were teenagers now. The family was in the process of immigrating to the United States. The Haas family, also from Czechoslovakia, was one that we became great friends with. They had six children, two of whom were Elvira and Anneliese. They encouraged me to attend the Israeli dancing class that was sponsored by NCSY, a Zionist organization. But that just wasn't my cup of tea. I was too self-conscious even to try, though I really enjoyed the melancholic and sometimes high-spirited Israeli melodies.

In addition to entertaining the young people in the camp, they would have been wise to also bring in a rabbi, orthodox, conservative, or reform, to be of aid to the traumatized, needy personalities. Such as, for instance, me. Many of the youngsters had been hidden children who were still searching for family members, and there were parents searching for their children, hoping that they hadn't perished in the concentration camps or on the road.

One day Papa found me reading a book about Count Dracula from Transylvania. He called the content *Schmutz und Dreck* and forbade me to read it. When he wasn't painting portraits, he tirelessly studied the English language, intending to make a worthwhile contribution to the country that adopts him: "Never to be a parasite, never a *Schmarotzer,* a freeloader!" Another priceless value he instilled in me. He was a great and loving teacher. Thank you, thank you, Papa! Can I ever say it enough?

Chapter 15
West Germany and Departure

FINALLY, GOOD NEWS! We were assigned to a one-room living space in the small village of Ottmarshausen on the outskirts of Augsburg, West Germany. The landlord was Herr Huber. He had a long list of restrictions in his hand that we were more than happy to abide by, such as removing shoes before ascending to the upstairs room, no guests, and no alcohol.

Behind our living quarters, a Catholic church stood on a hill, ringing its bells every hour, a reminder, it seemed, that without the help of the righteous Christians we could not have survived. I will always be grateful to those compassionate human beings in that *verloren,* hidden, little Bohemian village. They put their own safety in jeopardy and truly exemplified that we are all children of God and indeed our brother's keepers!

The Haas family that we had met at the refugee camp moved to that village as well. Elvira and I were close in age and attended high school together in Augsburg. Our transportation was the famous *Schwäbische Eisenbahne,* a train with a steam locomotive that seldom reached a speed of more than five or ten miles per hour, which didn't disturb us as we always had enough to chatter about. Just for fun, we used to jump off the train, walk alongside of it for a while, and then hop on board again. We would never speak of being Jewish and never mention our experiences surrounding our survival. Our focus was on the future and a new and better world.

Papa tirelessly journeyed to the American consulate in Munich to try to attain a visa for us, for the purpose of immigrating to America. He always returned disappointed, but never pessimistic. Because of his physical deficiencies, he needed an affidavit, someone to vouch for him, literally to be responsible for his livelihood in the new country. Tante Fanny was not able to provide that for him. She was willing to sign a promissory note but didn't qualify for reasons of not being financially stable enough as an aging widow. Mutti as well had problems. She was foolish enough to reveal that Tante Jenny died of tuberculosis, and now the spots on her lungs accompanied by her chronic cough were a concern for the doctors.

The Americans were afraid that we might be a burden on the welfare system, and who could blame them? But we were never freeloaders! Mutti could support us by working as a seamstress, and Papa would never run out of contracts painting portraits. America could do worse, I thought.

During the post-war years, America still had a very strict quota entry system that depended on one's birthplace rather than one's nationality. Since we were born in Czechoslovakia, which was now under Communist rule, the Czech quota had a long waiting list. By contrast, the refugee children quota was wide open. It made sense for me to seek admission to the country because I met the requirements to immigrate as a student. We were so naïve, so needy.

I don't understand this sudden recklessness of our government. Why didn't our politicians bend over backward for us, the Jews? It wouldn't have snapped their backs. The entire world was set against us, even to the point of collaborating with the Nazis. What about IBM's involvement with the Nazis during World War II, designing computers for them to round up Jews?

And what was our American government's reaction to that? They spoke with forked tongues just like Switzerland, France, and Sweden. Didn't they know about Hitler's evil schemes? Our government's inaction cost so many lives, hopelessly altering so many more and ruining the remainder of their days forever. IBM still thrives, disclaiming all responsibility for its disloyal war activities—traitors to their country.

One day we received a letter from Tante Anna Kohlman, her married name. Tante Anna was a widow with an only son Hans, who lived somewhere in Europe. She was excited about the prospect of a possible family reunion and was more than willing to guarantee for me a voucher to obtain a visa for traveling to Uruguay.

Immigration laws were less rigid to that country, and the probability of my parents gaining permission to join me at a later date was promising. Papa did research and found that temperatures in Uruguay for the warmest months were no more than seventy-five degrees, and for the coldest, about fifty. Perfect! Never too hot or too cold, similar to the conditions in San Francisco, California.

But my parents were hesitant about the inoculations for exotic diseases, such as malaria, cholera, and typhoid fever. Papa especially had misgivings. How could he forget the loss of his two brothers to those dreadful plagues, and as far as we knew, medical science hadn't discovered any miraculous cures for these afflictions. Mutti's opinion was that the health laws in that country were too lenient, and she also had visions of tarantulas, scorpions, snakes, and alligators lurking in Tante Anna's backyard. Eventually, my parents ruled out South America, and with that decision, my dreams of one day climbing the slopes of the Andes Mountains in Chile, exploring Brazil's rainforests, and riding horses on the pampas of Argentina, vanished.

One day in the year of 1949, after Papa returned from delivering one of the portraits to the officers' quarters, he suffered a serious heart attack at the prime age of forty-seven. After ten days, he was released from the hospital in Augsburg with a document stating that he was restricted from engaging in all physical activity until further notice. Yes, Papa eventually recovered and he was still full of compassion for his family, but his spirit, his incorrigible optimism, was depleted.

Mutti was employed in a garment factory as Papa gradually regained some of his physical strength. I graduated from high school in the year of 1950 with good grades, considering that I hadn't attended real school since the age of eight-and-a-half. My father's homeschooling was superior, and let's also give my meticulous Onkel Joseph some of the credit. I was so lucky that way.

My cousin Ewald turned out to be a whiz kid. No matter how many times we played checkers together, I could never win. Later he

Leah, age 16, for high school graduation.

attained a degree in Mathematics and in the years to come he held a position as a computer wizard for the transportation system in southern Germany. Ewald was always very spiritual. For a few years, he attended a synagogue in Munich and prided himself in having a menorah sitting in his front window. Perhaps he didn't pursue a higher level in Judaism because he was never to have descendants to inspire him.

He decided that our world was not *Menschlich* enough to expose a child's soul to the dangers that may still lay ahead. Many years ago,

Mutti, my mother, in West Germany, in 1947.

Ewald also received the honor of being the chess champion of southern Europe.

Mia married into a wealthy family who were the owners of a tour
bus chain in Bavaria, Germany. Their family was of the Catholic faith.
I also have a cousin Martin, who was born after the war in West Germany. He tells you in no uncertain terms that he is an atheist and that
"man is an accident of nature, a cosmic fluke!"

The last few weeks before my departure were happy ones. My
grandparents planned to flee Russian-dominated Czechoslovakia via

*Papa, Onkel Zeph, and Mama going for a stroll
in the city of Augsburg in 1949 or 1950.*

Switzerland. They joined us in West Germany. My dear Mama, my grandmother, lovingly tailored a suit by hand for me to wear on the journey to America.

I am not sure to this day that my parents, who were so overprotective all those years, were wise to let me immigrate to a strange land alone, considering how naïve and unsophisticated I was. Didn't they realize that I still needed their guidance? They should have listened to Mama, who didn't approve of my departure. Perhaps my Papa was overwhelmed with my Mutti's depressive state and its consequences? May they all rest in peace! They meant well.

Only Papa accompanied me on the celebrated Orient Express on our way to Cherbourg, France. Mutti couldn't bear to bid another *Servus,* another farewell. On the way, we passed so many fields of purple lavender. The aroma was so pleasing! We had a three-day layover in

Papa and his brother Zeph, in 1950.
Zeph survived one of Hitler's work camps.

Paris, where we reminisced in the cafes on the banks of the Seine about all our past experiences. So many agonizing, bittersweet memories, so many regrets!

A couple of thousand meters from the shores of Cherburg, France, the ocean liner *Queen Elizabeth* appeared like a mirage in the twilight, floating eerily in the vast English Channel. It looked fictitious. My head was spinning and I was holding my breath again. I barely said a proper goodbye to Papa. A smaller vessel took me and many others to the ocean liner that soon loomed like an impressive skyscraper in front of me.

I traveled tourist class, third class, which meant that my cabin was well beneath the portholes, just above the roaring engines of the craft. For five days, I suffered agonizing nausea day and night. Only twice did I drag myself up the endless stairways to the deck for a breath of

Tante Minkl and Tante Erna's advice:
"Keep smiling and behave yourself!"

fresh air. And only once did I have the courage to visit the dining area, where I noticed to my dismay that the tables and chairs were secured to the floor with chains.

America!

On the last day of the voyage, hundreds of passengers on deck anxiously awaited a glimpse of Manhattan Island, the "Land of the Free!" The New York skyline slowly became visible in the distance, and as we came closer, we saw another apparition. The Statue of Liberty, in the middle of New York Harbor, a gift from the French!

Finally, the anchor was dropped. A smaller craft transported us to Ellis Island, where I attached myself to endless lines of passengers. An immigration officer asked me countless questions and, in the process, they mistakenly changed my middle name. Some passengers were

Leah, age 17, at the Munich Consulate in the suit that Mama made, ready to depart for the "Promised Land" in 1951.

diamond-bedecked and others wretched, like me. My new suit, made by my grandmother, was wrinkled, and my hair was stringy and disheveled. I applied no lipstick, and my face was dotted with blemishes. I was nauseous again, perhaps out of fear or maybe because I hadn't eaten a meal in several days. What a sight I must have been!

After hours of endless questions by the immigration officers, where they falsely recorded a middle name of Erna on my passport, I finally made my grand entrance through the gate. America, here I am! I tried to imagine my great-aunt's appearance. Amongst hundreds of patiently waiting people, I spotted a pale little lady, about 4'8", who resembled Tante Minkl. She smiled and hesitantly waved. "Could that tall, untidy girl be my sister Auguste's granddaughter?" she probably asked herself. We introduced and greeted each other and proceeded to board a bus headed for Camden, New Jersey. Tante Fanny lived frugally in a two-bedroom flat near a synagogue that we attended only twice while I lived with her, though she never failed to light the Shabbat candles. In later years I discovered that the name of the head of the *shul*, the synagogue, was Rabbi Naftali Riff Gettinger, whose grandson years later became rabbi of the Hebrew Orthodox Shul in South Bend, Indiana.

Tante Fanny and I were a mismatched pair. She was not at all outgoing, and I was an introvert with few talents in the field of domestic chores, such as cooking or cleaning, which might have impressed that old-fashioned little lady. I noticed that she was decidedly unlike her sister, my grandmother. Each time she addressed me, it was with a hint of sarcasm, and a warm smile seldom crossed her face. There was no *Familiengefühl*, family feeling, between us. A *verbissene*, a grim little lady, perhaps embittered by the struggle for survival in the *Goldene Medina*. May she rest in peace.

Within a few days, Tante Fanny's daughter Gertie paid a visit. She asked dozens of questions, and each time I spoke, she laughed and snickered. I spoke with a British accent, and she found that amusing. Tante Fanny and Aunt Gertie told me in no uncertain terms that I had to learn how to work before I could even consider attending college.

She made arrangements for a job in a restaurant, washing dishes. I had never seen so many huge, crusty pots and pans. It was overwhelming! By the end of that first day, I was dismissed.

Tante didn't give up. I was hired by one of her lady friends to do ironing. Did I know how to iron? Of course not! I was familiar only with the irons we used to heat on top of the old iron stoves, and I had never used one before. Not that I didn't sincerely try, but I was literally engulfed by the mounds of ruffled curtains, left burn marks on a couple of lady's blouses and men's starched shirts. The ladies only expressed negative opinions about my efforts. Aunt Fanny said I brought shame upon her. Next on the list was a sewing factory position, which was more familiar, more agreeable. The minimum wage was forty-five cents per hour, and I tirelessly held that position for six months.

Life was not easy on the American soil. Where was the milk and honey? I was used to walking, so the seven blocks to and from work were therapeutic. On my way homeward from the garment factory in Camden, New Jersey, I usually strolled slowly in the dark, gazing longingly into well-lit windows facing the streets and occasionally catching a glimps of family gatherings, wishing I were home again with my parents, my grandmother, Tante Minkl, and Ewald.

Because I lived in a multicultural society in Bohemia, Czechoslovakia that respected and admired another's values and heritage, I found Tante Fanny's neighborhood quite fascinating: children happily playing ball in the streets, vendors selling newspapers and hot dogs in little carts, candy stores, and many "Mom and Pop" stores that displayed colorful clothing.

I had never seen so many "Moors" before! They were as friendly as I was, but Americans cruelly called them Negroes or *Schwartzes* or worse in the 1950s and '60s. One day I befriended myself with a girl about my age. She was fascinated with my accent and invited me to come to her home to meet her family. I thought that I should have Aunty's permission. When my Aunt saw the dark-skinned girl coming through her door, she could hardly keep her composure and contain her apparent disgust. She said "No" in no uncertain terms.

The next day her daughter, Aunt Gertie, appeared with her guns loaded. She told me to pack my meager belongings, and all the way to Woodbury, New Jersey, my new home, she lectured me about my inappropriate behavior in "hanging out with these people."

The following day, Aunt Gertie decided to change my apearance, which apparently she didn't approve of. She cut my hair very short, gave me a curly home perm, and plucked my dark thick eyebrows into a thin, straight line. I cried myself to sleep that night.

I faithfully wrote letters to my parents and promised to attend university as soon as I could. I don't believe that my parents had been aware that college was not free in the great country of America, nor was I informed that I was entitled to a government grant.

With these early experiences, I was indoctrinated into the American way of life, the melting pot of the world, that was, in my opinion, insensitive, if not revolting! Yes, in that era, everyone was struggling financially. The gap between the rich and the poor was wide, just as it is today all over this American land.

I eventually met and married a very handsome American soldier and moved to Batavia, New York. Seven years later, my parents finally received permission to immigrate to America, thanks to my generous physician, Dr. Mansueto of Batavia, who signed an affidavit guaranteeing my parents a position with his firm. He was a real Mensch who saw that his signature would reunite our family from across the wide Atlantic Ocean!

God bless America and the exemplary generosity of its people!

My father, Julius Peska, in the United States.

Chapter 16
Recapturing Judaism

PAPA WAS IN POOR HEALTH PHYSICALLY. He was also disillusioned by the frivolous American lifestyle and concerned with the
permissive movement by the young crowd in the 1960s and '70s,
which was encouraged by Dr. Spock. The distribution of drugs was
common among teenagers. Papa sadly predicted a couple of lost generations as an outgrowth of that dilemma. He also feared that our
American government under a fanatic leadership could usher in a
change of philosophy and an eventual recurrence of anti-Semitism.

"God is dead!" Papa said and advised us not to get involved in politics or religion, based on humanity's evil deeds. "How could God have
allowed so many unspeakable tragedies to happen?" He as well was
disillusioned by the countless *-isms*, such as Imperialism, Humanism,
Socialism, Communism, Fascism, Neo-Naziism, and even, unfortunately, Judaism. Neither was he impressed with Capitalism getting
"out of control" in Czechoslovakia or America.

Much as I idolized my Papa, I was disappointed that he did not
look inward and realize that a great deal of anti-Semitism started
when our Jews got involved in politics and governmental functions,
such as the Socialist movement that turned into Communism under
Stalin and turned out to be a ruthless dictatorship. This was the one
piece of advice I should not have taken, however well-intentioned it

no doubt was. My opinion is that, especially in America, if you do not belong to a religious or a cultural institution, you are lost and are subject to assimilation.

It was not until a few days before his decline that he all of a sudden recaptured his former *chachma*, spirit and wisdom, as if God had chased away the ghosts of the past. My Papa died of heart failure in the year of 1974. An irreplaceable human being, *Alav haShalom.* May my Papa rest in peace! He was my best friend!

My mother and I were devastated and lost without him. We had lived all these years in a world of our own, where no one knew of our past. My dear Mutti was clinically depressed and always kept her survival experiences deep inside and could not speak of them without crying. We should have attended Survivors meetings. It could have eased our "survivor's guilt," helped to heal my Mutti, and restored my self-confidence. I needed to grow up and take the awesome responsibility of our Jewish continuance seriously. The closest synagogue was in Batavia, New York, seven miles from our home town of East Pembroke. It was a conservative synagogue with an Orthodox rabbi.

Rabbi David Silverman was very special. He was sympathetic and supportive of our circumstances and so also were the twenty-five members of the Jewish community. Many experiences tormented me day and night for so many years. Some were a blotch on my Jewish soul. The rabbi assured us that we had no reason to feel guilty about anything. It was our duty to stay alive, to, God willing, produce Jewish descendants so Hitler would turn over in his grave. I tried to the best of my ability to keep my promise. If we had not made some of these daring, controversial choices to survive World War II, I wouldn't be here today and neither would the long list of my flourishing descendants who are a product of my values and my philosophies and our staunch belief in God, *Hashem*! And it may very well be that I am riding on the coattails of my offspring and that may well be true. My family had the determination, the endurance, the strength, the patience, and the opportunities to achieve what I couldn't.

Interestingly, I have observed that none of the Czechoslovakian Jews, with the exception of Madeline Albright, who was one of the hidden children, play major or minor roles in the political life of our country. Perhaps they haven't forgotten the bitter disappointments, failures, and life-threatening incidents that are the consequences of giving their hearts and souls to the diverse, schizophrenic governments, their leaders, and to the countless *-isms*. Possibly, the Bohemian Jew has come to realize that he was too attached to the soil. As with my dear parents, perhaps he sees that the Jewish soul needs spiritual nourishment and inspiration to be able to flourish and thrive.

In my dear mother's eightieth year, as an antidote for her unobservant past and as an overture of *T'shuva*, repentance, she created with charcoal pencils a dozen works of art portraying the Jewish holidays and customs. The warm and wonderful expressions she put on the faces of the Jewish subjects in her paintings are truly extraordinary. She was honored at an art exhibition at Sinai Synagogue in South Bend for her God-given talents. These precious mementos of love for her family will be treasured for generations to come. She was a beloved lady of incredible generosity and resilience, blessed be her memory. I am proud also of the two hundred blankets that she crocheted in her later years. These were raffled off for generous contributions to various local charities.

Some of my Papa's art is displayed in my living room. One day many years ago, around 1965, Papa called and excitedly told me of an article he found in a magazine of the University of Leipzig where they displayed a picture hanging in the auditorium. He immediately recognized the famous painting of the medieval fortress of Schreckenstein. In the foreground, a boat was crossing the river Elbe.

The passengers were none other than the symbols of the Bohemian culture, an artist, a musician, a poet, a dreamer-philosopher, and a peasant girl with a basket of herbs. Despite his poor eyesight he passionately recreated that priceless memory of that piece of earth, inhabited for hundreds of years by the Jewish people. How lucky I am to still have a token of my Mutti's and Papa's artistic talent and devotion, absolute loyalty, and perpetual optimism.

My Papa was an extraordinary human being. Listen to this priceless memo he scribbled in German while he was confined to bed!

> One acquires the virtue of wisdom in the declining years.
> Man begins to look within himself. One thinks and acts
> responsibly, realistically, and clearly.

If you keep a record of years gone by, you may be
    disillusioned and disappointed and realize that life
        is a never-ending struggle for survival.
Ambitions, aspirations, challenges, and urges melt away.
    Ideals and visions disappear into gray clouds.
        One sees reality, has experienced lives, conflicts,
            and has become a keen observer of mankind.
Joy and sorrow alternate like ebb and tide.
    The past appears to me like a
        kaleidoscope of brilliant colors.
Childhood memories are awakened, and one relives
    the comforting atmosphere of the parental home,
        regardless of how impoverished the existence.
We sat on the shores and tried to look beyond the horizon
    with our hearts filled with a better world to come.
        And then suddenly, we were overwhelmed
            by the seriousness of life.

Recently I found another note written by Papa, presumably just before his decline, and each time these precious notes are like a gift from
Sh'mayim, heaven. I translated his poem to the best of my ability:

It must be the onset of old age
    that makes my thoughts turn to prayer,
        that makes me want to daven, to thank Hashem
            for every precious day he graces me with.
And when Hashem grants me the pleasure
    of waking again in the morning,
        I am grateful, regardless of how I feel
            or how many anxieties plague my thoughts.
Each day makes me feel that I am born again,
    which renews my confidence that Hashem
        may again let me enjoy yet another day.

Doesn't it resemble the morning prayer in the *Chumash*? Impressive. Apparently, my Papa was a religious man after all!

148

Epilogue

THE GLOBAL COMMUNITY now finds itself in the year 2019. The hypocrisy and irrelevance of the news delivery, the hype on TV, is most of the time a contradiction of what is really happening in the world, in Israel, in Iraq, in Iran, in Russia, in Africa, and in South America. I see the comparison and the connection between those dictatorships, the common oppression, and methods of manipulation and control. And again I find myself under the spell of the Hitler syndrome.

The past seems to be catching up with the present. We are witnessing the same labor pangs now as then. We are caught up in the same spiritual crises here and in Israel, now, as then in Bohemia. Judaism encounters in all the corners of the world the same hostile reactions. The children of Israel must again fight for their lives, must again rise up not to one or two, but to countless madmen of astronomical proportions. Our enemies are keenly aware of the dangerous insights and doubts in the Jewish soul, and they have vowed to crush it, stamp it out, nip it in the bud!

We must remember that we haven't won the war yet. Jewish survival, and humanity in general, still hangs in the balance. We, the few remaining survivors of the Second World War and the Holocaust, as well as other victims of acts of inhumanity, must memorialize our testimonies, however insignificant, to assure the continuation of the dynamics and enthusiasm of the Jewish Spirit.

I will now complete my memoirs with loving words to the observant as well as to the secular members of my family.

Just like Abraham, we need to smash our graven images, our idols of materialism and articles of self-indulgence, that are obstructing the eyes of our souls. We don't know any more how to look at the world with fresh eyes of wonder, with the innocence of a child.

Perhaps we've been in the Garden of Eden all along? We only felt that we left it because we closed the eyes of our soul to it. By narrowing our vision, we entered into a self-imposed prison, and when you are in a state of narrow-mindedness you are not focusing on the whole picture. Small-mindedness breeds jealousy and greed, it sees destruction and cut-up pieces.

Broadmindedness sees a symphony in the making. As the saying goes, "God is in the details, but that is only true after you've seen the details within God." Power, truth, love, wisdom, kindness, and justice are just some of the qualities of reality. They do not pass on. They are timeless.

Which brings to mind this inspiring quotation: "We need all to have community consciousness. My behavior influences yours and your awareness sways mine. Without responsibility and commitment to each other there is no family, there cannot be a community."

I don't have to preach about compassion and kindness to my offspring. They all still have the innocence of children. They all are endowed with education of the heart and practice the values of Abraham in their daily lives. In fact, I have to remind them occasionally that kindness alone is not enough. It has to be moderated with truth, with reality.

Kindness alone can be harmful, because it can cause you to give in to someone's wishes, even in cases where it's wrong. You need to be well-balanced and honest with yourself, objective and unemotional, and no matter what your hereditary tendencies, no matter what environmental shortcomings you were exposed to, you have a choice. You can reach beyond and work on your inefficiencies and on your self-esteem. Only after we make the right choices do we fulfill our purpose and achieve wholeness.

I've been fortunate to be able to visit our precious land of Israel several times with my dear husband Robert Raphael Kabel, may he rest in peace. That piece of earth is our gift from God. We need to cherish it and defend it. More than half of our Jewish counterparts still live in exile, dispersed all over the world. We have the solemn responsibility to be a shining example of decency, integrity, and humility for the entire global community, to see and to guide them with open hearts and receptive minds.

I am very proud of my amazing four children, David, Sharon, Michael, and Reuven, who are the indirect victims of World War II and the Holocaust. My youngest son Reuven had the courage and determination to bring all of us all back into the Jewish fold and back to religion. David and Michael, my two oldest sons, have *goldene Hande* and with their artistic talents could have become architects under more supportive circumstances. My daughter Sharon was known as the "brain" of the family, was always on the honor role, won scholarships, and obtained an MBA from the University of Notre Dame.

My children have generously bestowed me with extraordinary grandchildren, Bekki, Nathaniel, Raquel, Aleeza and Avi, Jacob, Ari, and Justin, Jason, Josh, Jared, Courtney, and Troy, and the precious Nochschleppers, Eliyah and Ori. Bekki, Raquel, and Aleeza are shining examples of Bais Israel women. And let's not forget my admirable grandson-in-law, Rabbi Kuppel Lindow, my granddaughter Bekki's husband, and in addition my two delightful daughters-in-law, Susie and Reut. Reut is my Israeli member of the family. My cup runneth over already because, in addition, Hashem blessed me with beautiful multi-talented great-grandchildren, Yehuda, Shimon, Temima, Sarala, Bracha, Chana, Chaim Tzvi, Rochel, Sammy, and Rudy.

My gratitude goes to Hashem for bestowing me with a multitude of descendants that would not be in my midst if we had not survived the War, no matter how costly.

As a tribute to my dear mother and an opportunity to further glance into her soul, I'll close my thoughts with one of her favorite poems written by Börries Freiherr v. Munchhausen, printed in Berlin, Germany in the year of 1900. I will do my best to translate it from the German version into English. I assume that the poem indicates hope that Mashiach will appear on the Shabbath of Shabbathem.

Sabbath der Sabbathe

Sei still, Judaea, und scheige, Du Tochter des Sem!
Höere was ich dir sage:
Es nahet der Tag der Tage
Nach Streben und Sterben und Streit,
Nach Lieben und Lehren und Leid
Nahet die Ernte der Saat
Der Shabbath der Shabbathe naht!

Sei still, Judaea, und schweige, Du Tochter des Sem!
Hange deine Hoffnung ans Später,
Traue dem Gott der Vater!
Aus Zeiten voll Schande und Spott
Fuhrt dich dein heiliger Gott
Mit unerfoschlichem Rat:
Der Shabbath der Shabbathe naht

Shabbath of Shabbathem

Be silent, Judea, and hold your tongue, you daughter of Shem!
Listen to what I say:
The day of days is near.
After striving and fighting and dying,
After loving and teaching and grieving,
The harvest of seeds is approaching:
The Shabbath of Shabbathem is near!

Be silent, Judea, and hold your tongue, you daughter of Shem!
Hang your hopes on the future,
and trust the God of your Fathers.
Out of endless times of shame and mockery,
your holy God will lead you with impenetrable advice and guidance!
The Shabbath of Shabbathem is near!

Drawing by Sara Peska, my mother.

*Rabbi Menachem Mendel Schneerson was hailed
as the most famous "outreach" rabbi, one of the most
influential rabbis in modern history. In Russia,
Romania, Czechoslovakia, and Ruthenia, he
established pre-school classes and programs
and care-homes for the disabled.*

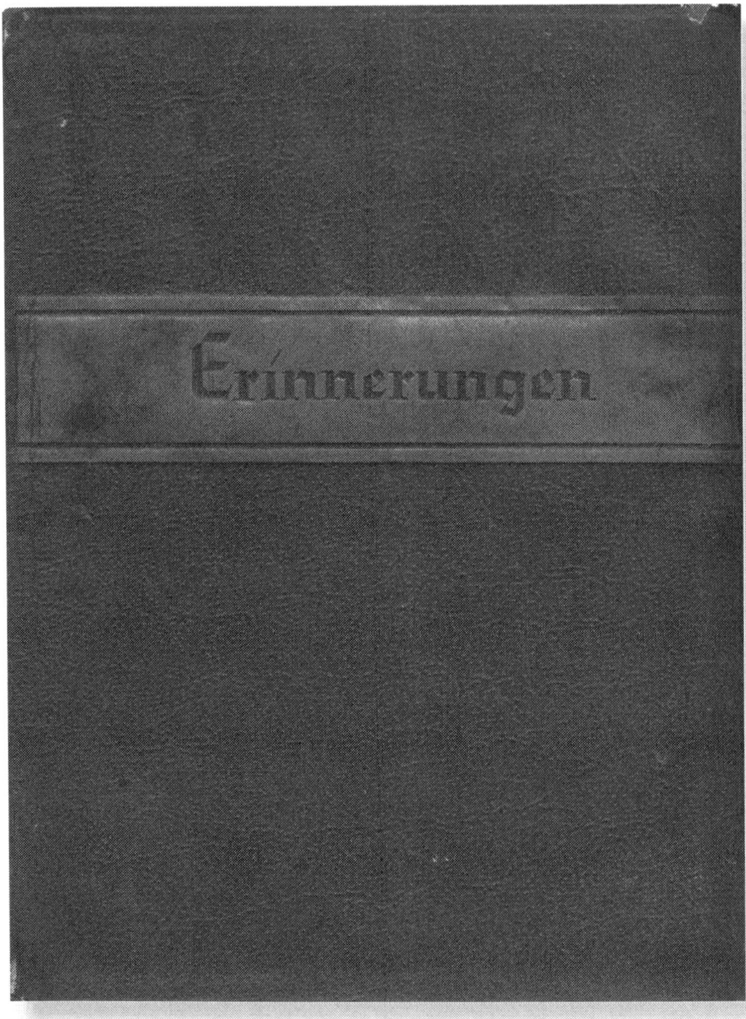
Erinnerungen

Remembrances

It was a custom—give it a look
Glimpses of the culture still survive
Passed-down wisdom
Personal expression of the ones
who lettered the thoughts
Treasure their handwriting
bound in a book

I believe it might have been a tradition carried on in most European countries to keep a diary of sorts, just as Anne Frank did so long ago in Amsterdam. Not just of daily occurrences, but of hand-drawn pictures of flowers or castles from your friends and school companions, letters of endearment from relatives brimming with good advice, and philosophical poems. To this day, I've treasured my priceless book of memories from my family members, living and departed, like a precious jewel, through good times and bad, close to my heart.

*My dear parents presented me with a diary
as a farewell gift at my departure to America:*

Dearest Daughter!
*May this book always be a good friend to you, in happy
or gloomy days. You can confide in it your most beautiful
memories, experiences, or impressions, as well as your
valuable acknowledgements, your designs, your resolutions,
your aims in life, your intimate thoughts and feelings.*

*Bestowed to you by your parents
in deepest never-ending love.*

My great-grandmother Shoshanah's sentimental words:

Let the sun shine into the fleeting years of childhood
Luminous ray of childhood, you are the one
who radiates warmth in the declining years.

1940

My grandfather Tate's wise words:

Don't judge too quickly the character,
the worthiness of a human being.
On the surface, there may be turbulent waves,
but the pearl lies at the depth of the ocean.

Aussig, 1941

Wilst du glücklich sein in Leben,
Trage bei zu Andrer Glück,
Denn die Freude, die wir geben,
Kehrt ins eigene Herz zurück.

Zur Erinnerung und in
aller Liebe,
deine
Großmutter.

My dear grandmother Mama's advice:

If you want to be happy in life,
Contribute to another's well-being.
For the joy and delight we give one another
Will return to your own heart.

Profound phrases written by my persnickety Uncle Joseph:

My dear niece Liane!
You were born like all of us, a creature full of potentiality. The more skilled and mature you become, the more accountable and responsible you will be in shaping your character. I therefore call to you, "Create successfully, Soul, Spirit, and Body!" And consequently, may my best wishes accompany you!

1945

Ob die Zeit auch hingeflogen,
Die Erinn'rung weichet nie;
Als ein lichter Regenbogen
Steht auf trüben Wolken sie.

Zur Erinnerung an deinen
Cousin
Ewald Dörfler

17. Februar 1953

My cousin Ewald's sentimental lines
at age eleven:

Though the time flew by quickly,
The memories will never fade away.
Like a luminous rainbow
They light up the gloomy sky!

1953

161

So wie Aussig-Teplitz beide
Schwesterstädte eng verbünden
Tun wir zwei uns nichts zuleide
Hab'n in Freundschaft
                                   uns gefünden.

Just as the sister cities of Aussig-Teplitz
are closely connected,
We have found each other in friendship
to never offend each other.

Christi Barber

Viel denken wenig sagen
Seine Not nicht jedem Klagen
Sich in Glück u. Unglück schicken
Ist eins der grössten Meisterstücken

„Was Du tust
das tue ganz
in der Halbheit
Liegt Kein Glanz!

Betty Heuberger

Zur steten Erinnerung
von deiner Mitschülerin
Betty Herthenstein v(Heuberger

Ottmarshausen
den 24.12.
1952

Do lots of thinking, not much talking,
Don't share your grief and despair.
Accepting good and bad luck with defiance
Is one of the great human skills.
What you do, do in full.
No glory in going half the way.

In constant memory, your classmate,
Betty Herthenstein von Heuberger

Ottmarshausen, 1952

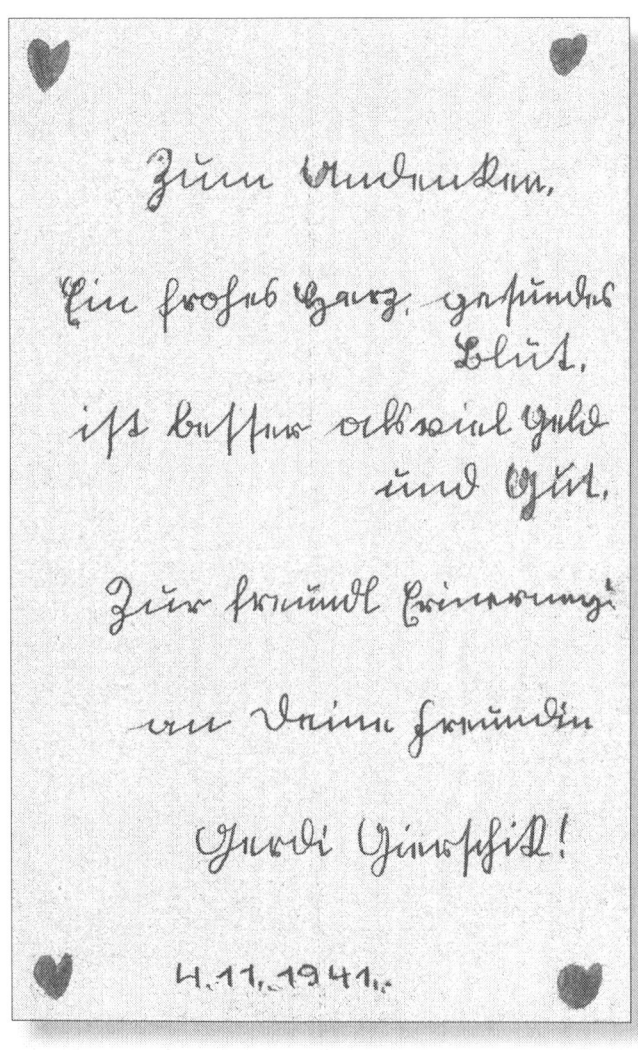

A body of health
A heart of gold
A soul full of spirit
So you can defy suffering

Gerdi Gierschick

1941

164

O, nütze der Jugendzeit fröhliche Stunden

Sie wissen nichts von Wiederkehr

Einmal entflohen, einmal entschwunden,

Zurück kehrt keine Jugend mehr.

Zur steten Erinnerung

an Deine Mitschülerin

Hanna Loibl

Königsbrunn, den 8. März 1949

O, utilize the years of your youth
  with happy hours,
They know nothing of returning.
Once flown away, once disappeared,
Youth will reoccur no more.

Your classmate
Hanna Loibl

Königsbrunn, 1949

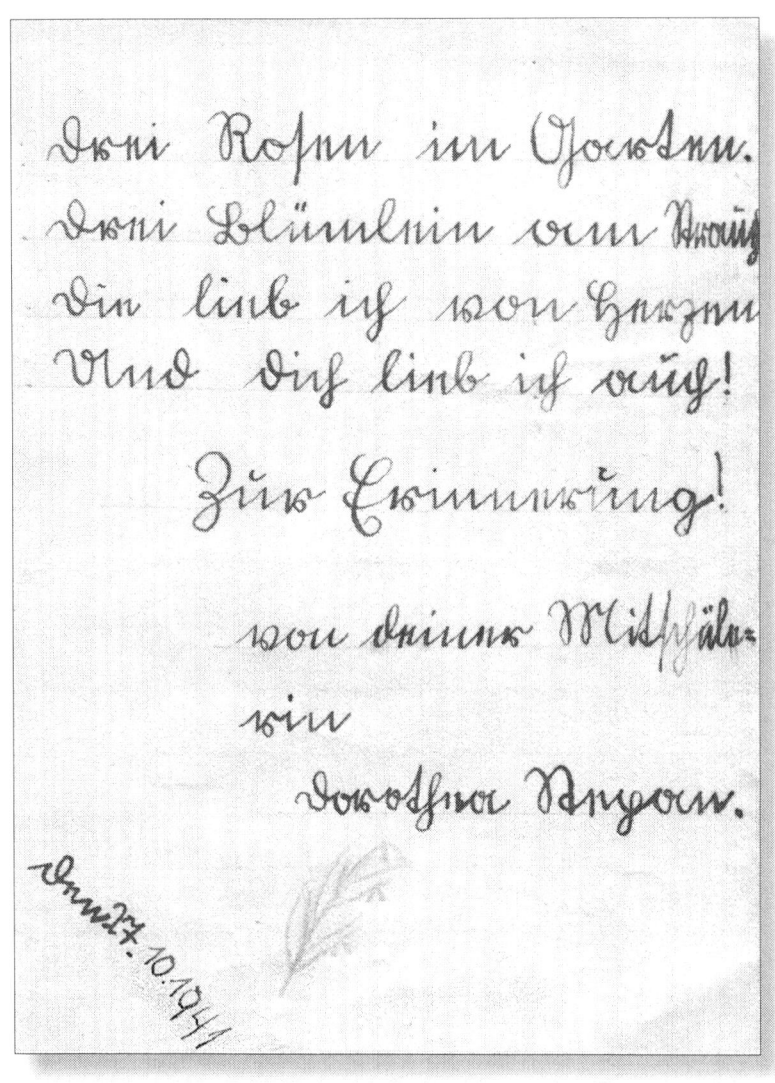

The days are like leaves in this book
Fill them with good deeds
And a remarkable pure lifestyle

Your classmate,
Dorothea Nesau

1941

Three roses in the garden,
three flowers in the meadow,
I love with all my heart
and I love you too!

In remembrance,
your friend Mara

Die Rosen sind ja Blätter
nur, Im Buche deines Lebens;
füll sie mit guten Taten aus
Und Machen meine Werbung!

Von deiner
Schülerin
Gerdi Grubin.

Leipzig am 26. Juni
1941

Three roses in the garden
Flowers from the wreath I love
And I love you too!

Gerdie Gruben

1941

168

Kühn handelt jedesmal
der Gott berufene;
ich hab's gewagt, ist sein
Wahlspruch, nicht darf ich?
kann ich? wer steht mir bei?
wird's auch werden?
Sonst geschähe in der Welt nichts.

Zur Erinnerung

an Fam. Döhmling

Ottmarshausen, 20. 12. 51

Daring is the servant of God, such as the priest and rabbi.
"I said it" is his choice of words. "I dared to do it."

Do not say, "May I?" But, "Can I? Who will stand by me?"
These actions and words make things happen in the world.

In remembrance of the family Döhmling

Ottmarshausen, 1951

My precious, loving relations and friends
spoke during my formative years of kindness,
generosity, spirituality, and logical thinking.
Their words will inspire me forever.

Descendants

STRANGE AS IT MAY SEEM, I offer a sincere thank you to the Burgermeister, despite the fact that he was a fascist. He and Onkel Franz warned my Papa that he had been declared a #1 enemy of our district. That warning gave us time to falsify birth documents and destroy evidence of our Jewish heritage, as I stated before.

Hashem gave my Tante Erna, may she rest in peace, the opportunity to contact Father's cousin, Stienek Peska, to arrange for a hiding place in a remote Bohemian village between the years of 1942 and 1945.

Thanks to the Czech secret agents who volunteered to return from England to ambush and kill Reinhard Heydrich. Hitler had ordered him to round up the Czech and German Jews of Czechoslovakia.

Our gratitude to Pater Hladikova for risking his life to protect our Jewish family. Had we been discovered by the Gestapo, they would have herded the whole village into the chapel and burned it to the ground, as they had done in France and in Russia.

Once again our admiration and love to amazing Tante Erna, who managed at the American Embassy to secure a visa to cross into the American-occupied zone of West Germany and to the free world.

Because of these humane beings, we survived the long years of the Holocaust and lived to create precious and beloved descendants. Many are introduced on the following pages.

172

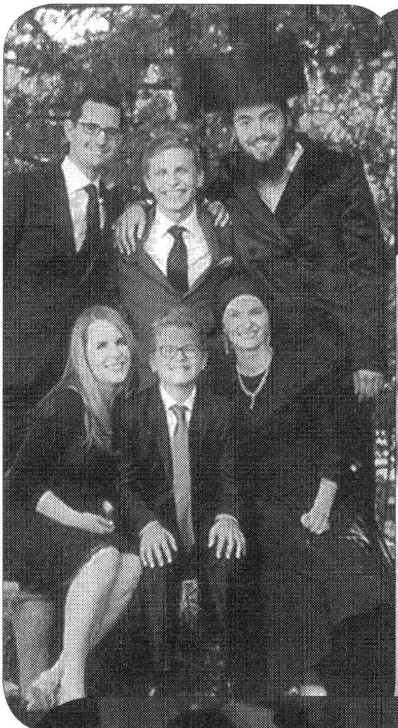
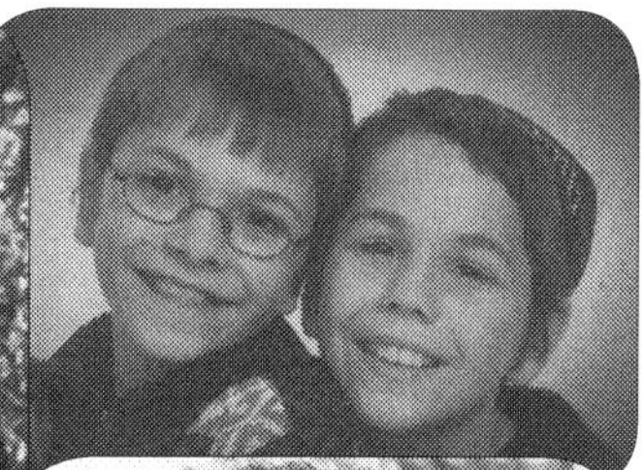
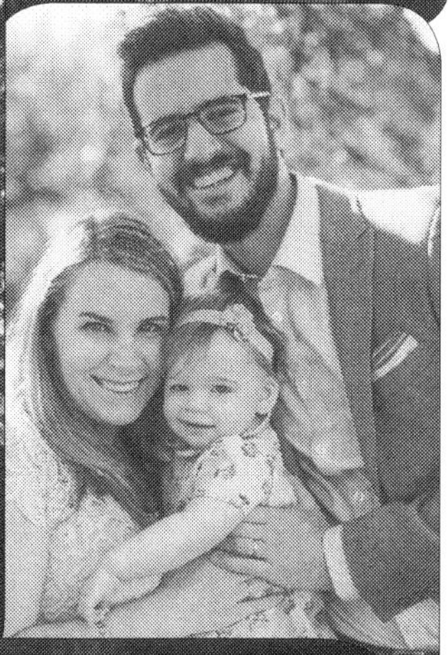
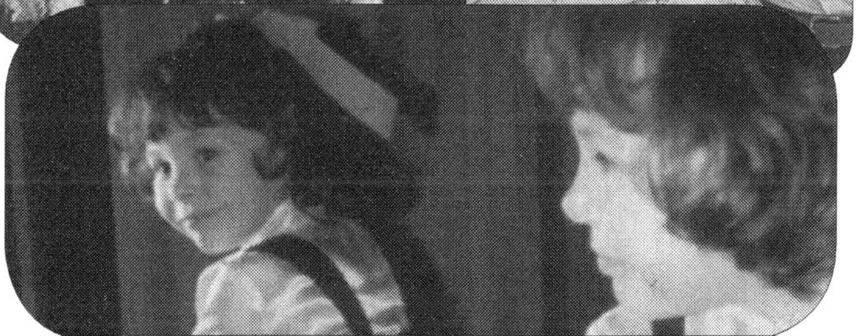
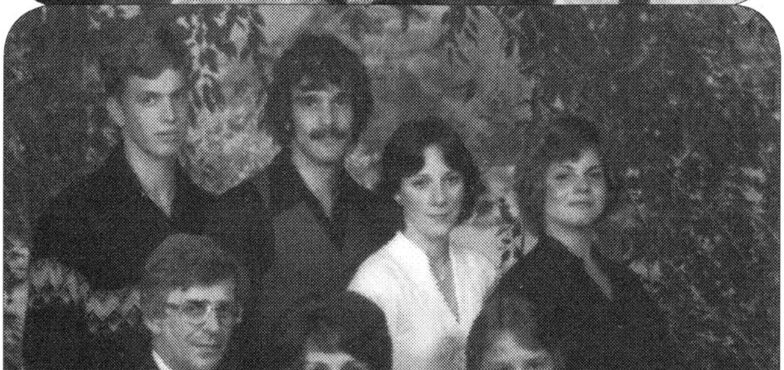

We will go on and on, celebrating family,
the dear grandchildren and great-grandchildren,
some not pictured here, others yet to be born,
all the grateful years of generations.

After risking everything to hide his cousin's
family, Stienek Peska survived the war.
He remained in his homeland, and
his descendants live there today.

Made in the USA
Columbia, SC
12 January 2020